The Seamless Ledger: Navigating the Digital Shift in Accounting

Unlock Efficiency and Compliance in Your Accounting Practices with Ease and Without Breaking the Bank

The Seamless Ledger: Navigating the Digital Shift in Accounting

Tommy W. George

Published by Tommy George, 2024.

THE SEAMLESS LEDGER: NAVIGATING THE DIGITAL SHIFT IN ACCOUNTING

First edition. April 18, 2024.

ISBN: 979-8224259038

Written by Tommy W. George.

Table of Contents

I am immensely grateful for the wisdom shared by fellow entrepreneurs and accounting professionals whose stories and advice have enriched these pages. Their willingness to explore new horizons and challenge the status quo has been a beacon of inspiration.

To my readers, thank you for embarking on this journey with me. Your commitment to growth and improvement is a testament to your dedication to excellence in your profession. This book is designed for mid-level to senior accounting professionals and business owners who are ready to transform their accounting practices but may feel daunted by the prospect. There are no prerequisites other than an open mind and the willingness to explore new possibilities.

The Seamless Ledger: Navigating the Digital Shift in Accounting

Unlock Efficiency and Compliance in Your Accounting Practices with Ease and Without Breaking the Bank

Preface

"The only thing that is constant is change." - Heraclitus

Chapter 1: The Digital Imperative: Why the Future of Accounting is Now

Embrace the Future or Fall Behind

Uncover the transformative power of digital accounting by exploring the pitfalls of sticking with outdated methods...

Chapter 2: Demystifying the Cost of Going Digital

Shattering the Myths of Digital Transformation Costs

Continue Reading: Learn how to effectively manage the transition to digital accounting with economical resources.

Chapter 3: Navigating the Minefield: The Dire Costs of Non-Compliance

The High Price of Ignorance: Why Compliance Cannot Be Overlooked

Explore how digital accounting can automate compliance processes and reduce risks...

Preface

"The only thing that is constant is change." - Heraclitus

In an era where digital innovation continually reshapes the landscape of industries, accounting stands at the precipice of a monumental shift. This book navigates the intricate journey of transitioning from traditional accounting practices to a modern, digital-first approach. It aims to demystify the complexities and illuminate a path toward enhanced efficiency and compliance, all without the daunting financial burden often associated with such transitions.

My decision to write this book was sparked by witnessing the struggles faced by numerous accounting professionals and business owners. Their battles with outdated systems, the relentless pace of regulatory changes, and the fear of integrating new technologies resonated deeply with me. Coming from a background where adapting to change was not just a choice but a necessity for survival, I felt compelled to share insights that could empower others to embrace transformation confidently.

I remember vividly, a conversation with Sarah, a seasoned accountant who expressed how manual processes were not just slowing her down but also leading to errors that cost her firm both money and reputation. Then there was James, a small business owner drowning in paperwork, unable to focus on growing his business because he was too busy trying to keep up with financial records. Their stories are not unique but rather a reflection of a widespread challenge that demands attention.

Drawing inspiration from my journey—from the turmoil of civil unrest in Liberia to establishing successful businesses and leading a thriving community in Virginia—I've learned the invaluable lessons of resilience, adaptability, and the power of faith and hard work. These experiences, coupled with practical business insights, have shaped the foundation of this book.

I am immensely grateful for the wisdom shared by fellow entrepreneurs and accounting professionals whose stories and advice have enriched these pages. Their willingness to explore new horizons and challenge the status quo has been a beacon of inspiration.

To my readers, thank you for embarking on this journey with me. Your commitment to growth and improvement is a testament to your dedication to excellence in your profession. This book is designed for mid-level to senior accounting professionals and business owners who are ready to transform their accounting practices but may feel daunted by the prospect. There are no prerequisites other than an open mind and the willingness to explore new possibilities.

By embracing the principles outlined in this book, you can expect to streamline your accounting processes significantly. The journey toward automation, cloud computing integration, enhanced data analysis, and foolproof compliance is within reach. More importantly, this path leads to liberating your time and resources so you can focus on what truly matters—growing your business and nurturing your team.

Thank you for choosing this book as your guide. Continue reading to discover how you can navigate the digital shift in accounting with ease and unlock efficiency and compliance in your practices without breaking the bank. Let's embark on this transformative journey together.

Chapter 1: The Digital Imperative: Why the Future of Accounting is Now

The sun had begun its descent, casting a honey glow over the bustling cityscape. In the heart of this urban hive, nestled within walls of glass and steel, sat Jameson, his figure hunched over a desk littered with papers. It was an island of antiquity in a sea of modernity. His fingers danced rhythmically on a calculator, punctuating the quiet hum of computers from neighboring cubicles.

Jameson had always prided himself on his meticulous nature, his ability to find order in numbers. But today, each tap on the calculator keys echoed like a drumbeat of obsolescence. He was aware that around him swirled digital solutions that could streamline his workflow, yet he clung to his manual methods like a captain to a sinking ship.

He paused and rubbed his temples as he pondered the ledger before him. A mistake – an errant digit misplaced in haste – now glared back at him accusingly. The error was small but significant; it was an emblem of the pitfalls lurking within outdated practices.

A colleague passed by, her tablet in hand, remarking on the latest cloud-based accounting software she had just implemented for her clients. "It's transformative," she said with enthusiasm that seemed foreign to Jameson's ears.

His mind wandered to what he had heard about digital accounting practices—the accuracy they promised, their efficiency. He envisioned himself freed from these piles of paper, from the drudgery that chained him to extended hours and constant double-checking.

A soft breeze wafted through an open window, carrying with it the sounds of life beyond these walls: laughter from a nearby park where children played without care for ledgers or balance sheets; the distant honk of taxis weaving through traffic like blood cells in arterial flow; somewhere out there life moved with fluidity that his own work lacked.

He turned back to his desk and eyed the computer that stood dormant at one end—a sleek machine capable of connecting him to realms of digital potential he had yet to explore. It offered an escape from this analog prison but required a leap into the unknown.

Could he adapt? Could he embrace this transition as not merely inevitable but as a gateway to new possibilities? The thought both excited and terrified him.

As twilight deepened and shadows crept across his office floor like silent specters, Jameson knew decisions loomed large over him. Would clinging to familiarity truly safeguard him or would it be the anchor dragging down his potential?

Outside, evening blossomed fully now; lights flickered on like stars being born in concrete skies. Perhaps tomorrow would be different—perhaps tomorrow he would join those who navigated by these new constellations of technology.

But tonight... tonight uncertainty remained as steadfast company as he gathered his coat and locked away secrets within drawers meant for another day's worry.

As Jameson stepped out into the crisp air that signaled day's end and night's beginning, one question lingered behind: When does adherence to tradition become a barrier rather than a bastion?

Embrace the Future or Fall Behind

In today's rapidly evolving business landscape, the transition to digital accounting is no longer an option but an imperative. The need for accuracy, efficiency, and compliance has never been more critical. As we delve into this essential journey, it's important to understand that clinging to outdated, manual accounting practices is a recipe for disaster. Errors, inefficiencies, and non-compliance with regulations are just the tip of the iceberg. This chapter aims to shed light on the urgency of adopting digital accounting practices and the transformative impact they can have on your business.

Understanding the urgency of this transition is crucial. The digital era has introduced a new set of rules in the business world. Financial transactions happen at lightning speed, data volumes are exploding, and regulatory requirements are becoming increasingly stringent. In this context, manual processes simply cannot keep up. They are too slow, too prone to error, and too opaque to ensure compliance effectively. The message is clear: adapt or risk being left behind.

But what exactly are the **pitfalls of sticking with outdated methods**? Beyond the obvious risks of errors and inefficiencies, there's a subtler yet more profound consequence: missed opportunities. In a world where data is king, manual systems offer little in the way of insights or analytics. They keep you reacting instead of proactively strategizing based on real-time financial intelligence. This lack of agility can be particularly damaging in today's fast-paced market environments.

On the flip side, embracing **digital transformation** presents a world of possibilities. It's not just about avoiding pitfalls; it's about unlocking potential. Digital accounting tools streamline processes, reduce errors to near-zero levels, and automate routine tasks. This not only frees up valuable time for strategic thinking but also ensures a level of accuracy and compliance that manual methods could never achieve. Moreover, cloud-based solutions offer accessibility and scalability that can transform how you do business.

Yet, for many, the path to digital may seem daunting. Concerns about cost, complexity, and learning curves are common roadblocks. However, this chapter aims to demystify these concerns by providing practical guidance on how to streamline your accounting processes and integrate technology solutions within 3 to 6 months without being overwhelmed by complexity or cost.

Reflecting on your current practices, ask yourself: Are they helping you thrive in today's digital economy or holding you back? Consider not only the immediate benefits of digital transformation but also its long-term impact on your organization's resilience and competitive edge.

By embracing an entrepreneurial spirit and leveraging strategic thinking and innovation, adopting digital accounting practices becomes not just feasible but invigorating. This journey requires hard work and dedication but promises significant rewards: more efficient operations, enhanced accuracy in financial reporting, ensured regulatory compliance, and ultimately a stronger financial position for your organization.

As we progress through this book, we will explore various aspects of digital transformation in accounting—from automation and cloud computing to data analysis and fraud prevention—providing you with comprehensive knowledge and practical tools to revolutionize your financial management practices.

Remember: The shift towards digital accounting is not merely a trend; it's a crucial step towards securing your organization's future in an increasingly complex and fast-moving business environment. Let this chapter serve as your starting point towards a more efficient, accurate, and compliant financial future.

In today's fast-paced business environment, the urgency of embracing digital accounting practices cannot be overstated. The shift towards digital solutions is not merely a choice but a necessity to stay competitive, efficient, and compliant in an increasingly complex financial landscape. **The traditional manual methods of accounting are quickly becoming obsolete**, unable to keep up with the demands of modern businesses that require real-time insights, data accuracy, and streamlined processes. **The future of accounting is now**, and those who fail to adapt risk falling behind and facing significant challenges in maintaining accuracy, efficiency, and regulatory adherence.

Digital accounting offers a plethora of benefits that can revolutionize the way businesses handle their financial processes. From cloud-based solutions that provide accessibility from anywhere at any time to automation tools that reduce human error and increase efficiency, the advantages of going digital are undeniable. **By embracing these technologies**, accounting professionals can elevate their roles from number-crunching to strategic advisors, guiding businesses towards sustainable growth and success. The digital imperative is not just about keeping up with trends; it's about future-proofing your business against potential pitfalls and ensuring long-term viability in a rapidly evolving landscape.

One of the key drivers behind the push for digital transformation in accounting is the need for enhanced accuracy. Manual data entry is not only time-consuming but also prone to errors that can have far-reaching consequences for a business. By leveraging digital tools such as automated reconciliation software and cloud-based platforms, organizations can minimize inaccuracies and discrepancies in their financial records. **The quest for precision in accounting practices is paramount**, as even minor errors can snowball into major discrepancies that may lead to financial losses or compliance issues.

Uncover the transformative power of digital accounting by exploring the pitfalls of sticking with outdated methods...

In today's fast-paced business landscape, clinging to outdated, manual accounting methods can be a recipe for disaster. **The pitfalls of sticking with traditional practices are numerous and can have detrimental effects on the efficiency and accuracy of your financial processes**. Imagine the frustration of dealing with piles of paperwork, manual data entry errors, and the constant fear of non-compliance with ever-evolving regulations. These issues not only consume valuable time but also open the door to costly mistakes that could harm your business in the long run.

Inefficiencies are a significant drawback of manual accounting methods. The time spent on repetitive tasks like data entry and reconciliation could be better utilized for strategic decision-making and business growth. Furthermore, manual processes are more prone to human error, leading to inaccuracies in financial reports and potentially damaging the credibility of your organization. **The risk of errors increases exponentially when relying on manual calculations**, putting your business at a higher chance of facing financial discrepancies and compliance issues.

Sticking with outdated accounting methods means missing out on the benefits of automation and digital solutions. Embracing digital accounting tools can significantly streamline your processes, reduce errors, and provide real-time insights into your financial performance. By continuing to rely on manual methods, you are essentially hindering your own progress and limiting your ability to compete in today's digital-first economy.

The consequences of not embracing digital accounting practices extend beyond internal inefficiencies. In a world where data security and compliance are paramount, manual processes leave your organization vulnerable to cybersecurity threats and regulatory fines. As regulations become stricter and data breaches more prevalent, it is crucial to prioritize digital transformation to safeguard your sensitive financial information and ensure compliance with industry standards.

Recognizing the pitfalls of sticking with outdated accounting methods is the first step towards embracing change. By acknowledging the limitations of manual processes and understanding the risks involved, you can pave the way for a smoother transition to digital solutions. It's essential to stay informed about the latest advancements in accounting technology and be proactive in implementing changes that will benefit your business in the long term.

Don't let fear or inertia hold you back from embracing digital transformation in your accounting practices. The future belongs to those who adapt and evolve with the times, leveraging technology to drive efficiency, accuracy, and compliance within their organizations. By recognizing the pitfalls of sticking with outdated methods, you can take proactive steps towards a more streamlined, secure, and future-ready approach to accounting that will set you apart in today's competitive business landscape.

In the digital age, the transformation of accounting practices is not just a luxury but a necessity. Embracing digital solutions is key to enhancing accuracy, streamlining processes, and ensuring compliance with regulations. By transitioning to digital accounting, businesses can unlock a myriad of benefits that go beyond mere efficiency. **Accuracy** in financial records is crucial for making informed decisions and projecting future growth. Digital tools provide real-time data analysis, reducing the margin for errors that manual processes often entail.

Furthermore, **streamlining processes** through digital transformation can lead to significant time and cost savings. Tasks that used to take hours or even days can now be automated, freeing up valuable resources for more strategic endeavors. This shift allows accounting professionals to focus on analyzing data and providing insights rather than getting bogged down in repetitive tasks.

Moreover, in today's regulatory environment, **compliance** is non-negotiable. Failure to adhere to financial regulations can lead to severe penalties and damage a company's reputation. Digital solutions offer built-in compliance features that help businesses stay on top of changing laws and regulations effortlessly. By leveraging these tools, organizations can ensure that their financial practices meet the required standards without the constant fear of non-compliance.

Digital transformation also enables businesses to future-proof their operations. As technology continues to evolve rapidly, those who resist change risk falling behind their competitors. By embracing digital accounting practices now, companies can position themselves for success in the long run. This proactive approach not only secures their current operations but also prepares them for future innovations in the accounting industry.

Ultimately, the role of digital transformation in accounting goes beyond mere convenience; it is about **strategic positioning** in a competitive landscape. Businesses that harness the power of digital tools gain a significant advantage over those still relying on outdated methods. The ability to access real-time data, automate processes, and ensure compliance gives them a solid foundation for growth and sustainability.

As you consider the benefits of digital transformation in accounting, think about how it can revolutionize your own practices. Imagine a future where you no longer have to worry about manual errors or compliance issues, where your time is freed up for more strategic initiatives, and where your business is prepared for whatever challenges lie ahead. Embracing digital solutions is not just a trend; it is a critical step towards securing the future of your business in an ever-evolving landscape.

In the rapidly evolving landscape of business, the shift towards digital accounting practices is not just a trend; it's a necessity. The urgency of this transition cannot be overstated. **Businesses that cling to outdated manual methods are not just falling behind; they're actively courting inefficiency, errors, and compliance risks.** By embracing digital transformation, organizations unlock a world of accuracy, streamlined processes, and regulatory adherence that was previously unimaginable.

Imagine the peace of mind that comes from knowing your financials are accurate and up-to-date, accessible from anywhere at any time. Picture the efficiency gains when manual data entry and reconciliation become things of the past. This isn't just a dream—it's the reality for businesses that have embraced digital accounting.

But why is this shift so crucial? At its core, it's about more than just keeping up with technology—it's about staying competitive in a marketplace where agility and insight hold the keys to success. It's about leveraging every tool at your disposal to ensure not just survival, but thriving growth.

For those ready to embark on this journey, the path ahead is filled with opportunities for innovation, growth, and strategic advantage. Each chapter that follows builds upon this foundation, offering practical tips, real-world examples, and strategies to make this transition not just painless but profoundly beneficial.

Embrace this journey with an open mind and a willingness to adapt. The benefits awaiting you—enhanced accuracy, improved efficiency, and ensured compliance—are just the beginning. As you turn these pages, allow yourself to be inspired by stories of triumph over adversity and invigorated by the promise of what's to come.

The future of accounting is digital, and the future is now. Let's navigate this shift together, unlocking efficiency and compliance in our accounting practices with ease and without breaking the bank. The road ahead is bright for those willing to take the first step.

Chapter 2: Demystifying the Cost of Going Digital

In the quiet calm of an early morning, before the city stirred to life, Martin sat at his desk. The soft glow of the computer screen was the only light in the room, casting shadows across his furrowed brow. He was a man caught between eras, one foot rooted in the tradition of ledgers and tax forms, the other stepping tentatively towards a digital dawn.

The air was still, yet charged with the silent energy of change. A mouse clicked, a single tap resonating through the room as Martin opened another spreadsheet. The numbers danced before him; they were an old friend and foe. He remembered his father's cautionary tales of businesses undone by change, yet here he was contemplating that very beast.

Martin's thoughts wandered to the myths he'd heard - that transitioning to digital accounting would be a financial chasm too wide to cross. His heart raced at the thought of such cost but was it fear or excitement? The scent of paper lingered in his office, a reminder of what had always been.

A soft chirp from his phone cut through his reverie. It was a message from Leah, a fellow accountant who had made the leap into digital realms months ago. Her words were always full of encouragement and practical advice on how to navigate this new world without being swallowed by expense.

He recalled her telling him about breaking down processes into manageable steps and investing wisely rather than widely. She spoke not just of user-friendly software but also of time saved and errors reduced – benefits that could be reaped in due time if only he dared to step forward.

Outside his window, dawn began to break; hues of orange and pink painted across the sky like an artist's canvas coming alive with hope and possibility. Martin watched as light spilled into every corner of his office, touching upon stacks of paper that seemed less comforting now.

He pondered over Leah's successes and wondered if perhaps there was truth in her words – that these initial costs were not walls but gates waiting to be unlocked. Could it be that embracing this change would lead not just to survival but also to flourishing?

As Martin weighed these thoughts against each other – fear against potential – he knew deep down that stasis was no longer an option. Change is like sunrise; inevitable and full of promise.

Will Martin find courage in Leah's example and take that decisive step towards transformation?

Shattering the Myths of Digital Transformation Costs

The journey into the digital realm, especially within the accounting sector, is often shrouded in myths of high expenditure and complexity. However, this narrative couldn't be farther from the truth. The essence of a cost-effective digital transition lies not in extravagant spending but in strategic, step-by-step implementation. By focusing on user-friendly accounting software and manageable process upgrades, organizations can embrace modern technologies without significant financial strain. This insight is crucial for businesses standing at the cusp of digital transformation, hesitant to take the leap due to misconceptions about cost and complexity.

Dispelling myths about the financial burdens associated with digital transitions is foundational to encouraging more organizations to embrace this change. The fear of unforeseen costs often acts as a barrier, preventing many from exploring the potential benefits of digital accounting solutions. It's essential to understand that with the right planning and resources, transitioning to a digital accounting system can be both straightforward and economically viable.

Learning **how to effectively manage the transition** with economical resources is another pivotal aspect of this journey. It involves identifying what your organization truly needs versus what is nice to have. Prioritizing core functionalities that enhance operational efficiency and compliance, without overinvesting in superfluous features, ensures that you're getting the most value for your investment. Additionally, leveraging cloud-based solutions can reduce upfront costs associated with hardware and maintenance, further debunking the myth that going digital necessitates hefty financial outlay.

The long-term **financial benefits** of adopting digital accounting solutions significantly outweigh initial setup costs. It's not just about digitizing existing processes; it's about reimagining how your accounting operations can be more streamlined, accurate, and efficient. With automation comes reduced manual errors, faster processing times, and improved compliance – all contributing to cost savings and enhanced profitability in the long run.

Imagine being able to access real-time financial data at your fingertips or automating repetitive tasks that once consumed hours of manual labor. These aren't just conveniences; they're transformative changes that can elevate your business's financial management and strategic decision-making capabilities.

Reflect on your current accounting processes. Are they as efficient and cost-effective as they could be? If not, it might be time to consider how a digital transformation could benefit your organization financially in both short-term implementation and long-term operational efficiency.

The entrepreneurial spirit thrives on innovation and strategic thinking. Embracing a digital shift in accounting practices embodies this spirit by leveraging technology to unlock new levels of efficiency and compliance. It's about making informed decisions that not only keep pace with technological advancements but also drive economic value for your business.

In navigating through this digital shift, remember that you're not alone. Many have successfully embarked on this journey before you, overcoming initial challenges through strategic planning and an openness to change. Their stories serve as testaments to the fact that with the right approach, transitioning to digital accounting is not only manageable but also financially rewarding in ways you might not have imagined.

By embracing these insights and strategies, you're well-equipped to demystify the cost of going digital in your accounting practices. The road ahead may seem daunting at first glance, but with each step forward, you'll discover that the benefits far outweigh the challenges - paving the way for a more efficient, compliant, and economically savvy future for your organization.

In the realm of accounting, the shift towards digital processes often carries a misconception of being prohibitively expensive. However, contrary to this common belief, transitioning to digital accounting doesn't have to break the bank. By dispelling myths about the high costs associated with going digital, organizations can embrace this change with confidence and efficiency.

One prevailing myth is that digital transition necessitates a massive initial investment. While there may be some costs involved in adopting new technologies, the long-term benefits far outweigh these initial expenses. **By investing wisely in user-friendly accounting software**, organizations can streamline their operations, reduce errors, and enhance overall efficiency. The key lies in understanding that the cost of not going digital may actually be higher in terms of time wasted on manual processes and potential errors.

Another misconception is that only large corporations can afford to go digital. In reality, there are numerous affordable accounting software options available tailored for small and medium-sized businesses. These solutions offer scalability, customization, and efficiency without the exorbitant price tags often associated with enterprise-level software. **Small businesses can leverage these tools to stay competitive** in today's rapidly evolving digital landscape.

Moreover, the fear of complex implementation processes can deter organizations from embarking on their digital transformation journey. However, with proper guidance and a systematic approach, the transition can be smooth and manageable. **Breaking down the process into smaller steps** allows for a more gradual and effective adoption of digital tools, minimizing disruption to daily operations.

It's crucial to recognize that the cost of going digital extends beyond monetary value—it encompasses time saved, reduced stress levels, improved accuracy, and enhanced decision-making capabilities. By shifting focus from short-term expenses to long-term benefits, organizations can overcome the fear of high costs associated with digital transition. **Ultimately, embracing digital accounting solutions is an investment in efficiency and sustainability** for the future of any organization.

Continue Reading: Learn how to effectively manage the transition to digital accounting with economical resources.

In the realm of digital accounting, it's crucial to understand that a successful transition doesn't always require a hefty financial investment. **By focusing on strategic planning and resource allocation**, organizations can effectively manage the shift to digital accounting without breaking the bank. One key aspect to consider is selecting user-friendly accounting software that aligns with your specific needs and budget constraints. **Investing in the right tools can streamline processes and enhance efficiency**, ultimately saving time and money in the long run.

When embarking on the journey towards digital transformation, it's essential to prioritize training and support for your team. **Ensuring that employees are equipped with the necessary**

skills to utilize new software can significantly impact the success of the transition. By providing adequate training sessions and ongoing support, you empower your staff to embrace change confidently and leverage digital tools effectively.

Another critical factor in managing the transition to digital accounting with economical resources is meticulous planning. Take the time to assess your current processes, identify areas for improvement, and establish clear objectives for the transition. By setting realistic goals and creating a detailed roadmap, you can navigate the shift strategically while minimizing unnecessary costs.

Consider leveraging online resources, webinars, and tutorials provided by software vendors to enhance your understanding of digital accounting solutions. These resources often offer valuable insights, tips, and best practices that can aid in a smooth transition without requiring substantial financial investment. **By proactively seeking knowledge and guidance**, you empower yourself to make informed decisions that benefit your organization's financial health.

As you navigate the path towards digital transformation, remember that every small step forward contributes to significant progress in the long term. **Celebrate achievements along the way**—whether it's successfully completing a training session or implementing a new feature in your accounting software. **Recognize the efforts of your team** and acknowledge the positive impact of embracing change within your organization.

In essence, managing the transition to digital accounting with economical resources is not just about cutting costs; it's about making strategic investments that yield substantial returns over time. **By adopting a proactive mindset**, embracing innovation, and prioritizing efficient resource allocation, you can pave the way for a seamless transition towards modern accounting practices. **Remember: every step taken towards digital transformation brings you closer to**

reaping the benefits of enhanced efficiency, accuracy, and compliance.

In the realm of accounting, the initial setup costs for transitioning to digital solutions can often seem daunting. However, it is crucial to shift our perspective and focus on the long-term financial benefits that these advancements can bring. By analyzing the return on investment over time, organizations can uncover significant savings, increased efficiency, and improved accuracy in their financial operations.

One of the key advantages of digital accounting solutions is the reduction in manual labor and human error. Automation features can streamline repetitive tasks, freeing up valuable time for employees to focus on more strategic activities. This not only boosts productivity but also minimizes the risk of costly mistakes that could arise from manual data entry.

Moreover, the accessibility and real-time nature of digital platforms allow for quick decision-making based on accurate and up-to-date information. This agility in responding to financial trends and challenges can give organizations a competitive edge in their industry, potentially leading to increased revenue and growth opportunities.

Another significant benefit lies in the enhanced compliance and security measures that digital accounting systems offer. By centralizing data storage and implementing stringent security protocols, organizations can mitigate risks associated with data breaches or non-compliance with regulatory standards. The potential financial repercussions of such incidents far outweigh the initial investment in secure digital solutions.

Additionally, digital accounting solutions often come with built-in analytics tools that provide valuable insights into financial performance. By leveraging these tools, organizations can identify cost-saving opportunities, optimize resource allocation, and forecast future trends with greater accuracy. This proactive approach to financial management can result in substantial long-term savings and improved overall financial health.

As organizations navigate the transition to digital accounting, it is essential to consider not only the immediate costs but also the lasting benefits that these advancements can bring. By embracing modern technologies and investing strategically in user-friendly software, organizations can position themselves for long-term success and sustainability in an increasingly digital landscape.

Embarking on the journey of digitizing your accounting practices might seem daunting at first glance. However, as we have explored together, the perceived high costs and complexities are often myths that can be dispelled with the right knowledge and approach. The truth is, with strategic planning and a focus on value over cost, this transition not only becomes manageable but also sets the stage for substantial long-term benefits.

Cost-effectiveness in digital transformation is not just a possibility; it's a reality that many organizations are already experiencing. By demystifying the initial setup costs and focusing on economical resources, businesses of all sizes have found ways to adopt digital accounting solutions without breaking the bank. This shift is not merely about upgrading technology; it's about embracing a mindset of innovation and efficiency that pays dividends far beyond the initial investment.

Remember, every organization's journey to digital adoption is unique. Yet, the stories of those who have triumphed over adversity by leveraging user-friendly software and breaking down the process into manageable steps serve as powerful testaments. These anecdotes underscore the attainability of making a seamless transition to digital accounting.

Have you considered how your organization can benefit from such a transformation? Reflecting on this question might reveal opportunities previously obscured by concerns over costs and complexity.

Moreover, analyzing the long-term financial benefits sheds light on how digital solutions can enhance not just efficiency but also compliance and decision-making capabilities. The initial effort and resource allocation become insignificant when viewed against the backdrop of improved accuracy, real-time data access, and strategic insights gained.

In navigating this digital shift, adopting an entrepreneurial spirit characterized by strategic thinking and hard work is crucial. Practical tips shared by those who've successfully made this transition highlight the importance of patience, perseverance, and continuous learning. Embrace these values, and you'll find that going digital is not just about keeping up with technological advancements but about fostering a culture of innovation within your organization.

Let this chapter serve as both an encouragement and a guide as you consider making the leap to digital accounting. With clarity, empathy, and an unwavering focus on long-term gains over short-term hurdles, your path to digital transformation will be marked by growth, efficiency, and resilience. Remember, in embracing digital solutions, you're not just changing how you manage your accounts; you're setting your business up for sustained success in an increasingly digital world.

Chapter 3: Navigating the Minefield: The Dire Costs of Non-Compliance

The sun hung low, a tired eye closing on the city's horizon. In the dwindling light, Martin sat at his desk, a fortress of paper and digital screens. His fingers danced across the keyboard with the precision of a pianist, yet each keystroke was a heavy note in the symphony of his anxiety. The new financial regulations were clear as day, but they felt like an obelisk casting long shadows over his company's future.

He recalled the conference room, walls lined with accolades of fiscal responsibility. They had all nodded in agreement then, unaware that their compliance framework was a house of cards waiting for a breeze. Now, as deadlines loomed like storm clouds, Martin's mind raced through scenarios where failure to comply meant fines that could bleed them dry or worse - erode their hard-earned reputation.

A ping from his computer snapped him back to reality. It was an email from Lydia in accounting; she had finalized integrating the new digital accounting system that promised salvation. The message read like gospel to Martin's beleaguered soul – automation would handle tax codes, transaction reports, and even alert them to regulatory changes.

Martin leaned back in his chair and let out a breath he didn't realize he'd been holding. He envisioned this digital sentinel working tirelessly while they slept, guarding against human error and oversight. His heart rate slowed as hope fluttered within him; perhaps this tool would be their shield in an arena where every misstep could be catastrophic.

As night took its claim on the office space around him, only Martin's desk remained an island under fluorescent light. He pondered how many others were out there right now grappling with similar fears? How many sleepless nights spent worrying about compliance?

He stood up and walked over to the window; it was dark outside now - just pinpricks of light from other offices where people like him fought their own battles against time and tide. The city breathed quietly below him – indifferent to the struggles within its glass towers.

Martin knew tomorrow would bring more challenges; it always did. But tonight he allowed himself a moment of peace as he imagined a world where digital solutions lifted burdens rather than added them. Was this what progress felt like?

As he switched off his monitor and prepared to leave the silent office behind for another night, one thought lingered: Could technology truly be trusted as the guardian against human fallibility in financial regulation?

The High Price of Ignorance: Why Compliance Cannot Be Overlooked

In the world of accounting, the landscape is shifting beneath our feet. With every passing day, digital technology is not just an option; it's becoming a necessity. The move towards digitization isn't just about keeping up with the times—it's a critical strategy for ensuring compliance with financial regulations. Non-compliance, as many organizations have painfully discovered, comes with severe implications. Fines, penalties, and reputational damage are just the tip of the iceberg. The real cost can be far more substantial, affecting an organization's very ability to operate.

Understanding the severe implications of non-compliance is crucial. It's not merely about facing financial penalties; it's about sustaining your organization's integrity and trustworthiness in a competitive market. Instances abound where companies have faced existential crises due to non-compliance issues that could have been avoided with more proactive financial management practices. These stories aren't just cautionary tales; they're stark reminders of what's at stake.

Discovering how digital accounting can automate compliance offers a beacon of hope in this challenging landscape. Digital solutions can streamline processes, reduce human error, and ensure timely reporting—all key components in maintaining compliance. But it's not just about automating tasks; it's about gaining insights that can lead to better decision-making and strategic planning. Digital accounting isn't just a tool for compliance; it's a pathway to enhanced efficiency and effectiveness in all areas of financial management.

Exploring strategies to implement digital solutions is where the journey begins for many organizations. It's one thing to recognize the need for digital accounting practices; it's another to successfully integrate these solutions into your existing operations. This requires careful planning, training, and perhaps most importantly, a willingness to embrace change. The goal is not just to meet current regulatory requirements but to future-proof your organization against upcoming changes in the financial landscape.

The entrepreneurial spirit thrives on innovation and hard work, and nowhere is this more evident than in the transition to digital accounting practices. By adopting these technologies, organizations are not just avoiding the pitfalls of non-compliance; they're setting themselves up for greater success in an increasingly digital world. Practical tips and real-world examples abound for those willing to take this leap, offering guidance and inspiration along the way.

As we delve deeper into this chapter, let's reflect on our own practices and consider whether we are doing enough to safeguard our organizations against the dire costs of non-compliance. **Are we proactive or reactive?** Are we leveraging technology to its fullest potential? These are not just rhetorical questions; they're invitations to embark on a journey toward better, more compliant financial management practices.

In navigating this minefield, remember that you're not alone. A community of forward-thinking professionals is rising to meet these challenges head-on, armed with digital tools and a determination to succeed. By joining this movement towards seamless compliance through digitization, you're not just protecting your organization—you're positioning it for unparalleled growth and success in the digital age.

Let this chapter serve as your roadmap through the complexities of compliance in today's fast-paced financial environment. With each step towards digitization, you're building a stronger foundation for your organization—one that stands on integrity, efficiency, and unwavering compliance.

Non-compliance with financial regulations can have dire consequences for organizations. The risks associated with failing to adhere to these regulations are not to be taken lightly. **Potential fines, penalties, and reputational damage** can severely impact the financial health and standing of a company. Moreover, the trust of stakeholders, including investors and clients, can be shaken, leading to long-term repercussions that may be challenging to overcome. In today's fast-paced and interconnected business environment, ensuring compliance with financial regulations is paramount to sustaining a successful operation.

The implications of non-compliance go beyond monetary fines; they extend to the very core of an organization's reputation and credibility. **Regulatory bodies** are becoming increasingly vigilant in enforcing compliance standards, making it essential for businesses to stay ahead of the curve. The fallout from non-compliance can tarnish a company's image, resulting in a loss of customer trust and loyalty. This erosion of goodwill can have lasting effects on the bottom line and future growth prospects.

Moreover, non-compliance can lead to a **ripple effect** within an organization. It can strain internal resources as teams scramble to rectify errors and address regulatory issues. The time and effort expended on remediation could have been better utilized in driving innovation and growth initiatives. Additionally, non-compliance can create a culture of uncertainty and fear within the organization, hindering employee morale and productivity.

As businesses navigate the complex landscape of financial regulations, embracing digital solutions becomes imperative. **Digitizing accounting processes** can streamline compliance efforts by automating tasks, ensuring accuracy, and providing real-time insights into financial data. By leveraging technology, organizations can proactively identify potential compliance gaps and address them before they escalate into larger issues.

In light of these severe implications of non-compliance with financial regulations, it is crucial for organizations to prioritize adherence to regulatory standards. By integrating digital solutions into their accounting practices, businesses can mitigate risks, safeguard their reputation, and ensure long-term sustainability. The path to compliance may seem daunting at first, but with the right tools and strategies in place, organizations can navigate this minefield successfully.

Explore how digital accounting can automate compliance processes and reduce risks...

In today's fast-paced business landscape, staying compliant with financial regulations is paramount for the success and sustainability of any organization. The consequences of non-compliance can be severe, leading to hefty fines, penalties, and irreparable damage to a company's reputation. However, the solution to this challenge lies in embracing digital accounting technologies that can automate compliance processes and reduce associated risks.

Digital accounting offers a myriad of benefits when it comes to ensuring regulatory adherence. By leveraging automation tools and software, organizations can streamline their accounting processes, minimize human error, and enhance the accuracy of financial reporting. This not only saves time and resources but also significantly reduces the likelihood of compliance violations.

Moreover, **digital solutions** provide real-time monitoring capabilities that allow businesses to stay ahead of regulatory changes and swiftly adapt their practices to remain compliant. Through automated alerts and notifications, organizations can proactively address any potential issues before they escalate into major compliance breaches. This proactive approach is key to mitigating risks and maintaining a strong foothold in an ever-evolving regulatory environment.

By embracing **digital transformation**, organizations can create a culture of compliance that permeates throughout all levels of the company. From top management to frontline employees, everyone can benefit from the transparency and accountability that digital tools bring to the table. This not only fosters a sense of responsibility but also instills confidence in stakeholders regarding the organization's commitment to following regulations.

Furthermore, **digitizing accounting processes** enables companies to generate detailed audit trails and maintain comprehensive records of all financial transactions. This level of transparency not only facilitates internal oversight but also provides external auditors with the necessary documentation to verify compliance with regulations. In essence, digital accounting acts as a safeguard against non-compliance by ensuring that every financial transaction is accurately recorded and easily traceable.

In conclusion, the shift towards **digital accounting** is no longer just a matter of convenience but a strategic imperative for organizations looking to navigate the complex landscape of financial regulations successfully. By automating compliance processes, reducing risks, and fostering a culture of accountability, digital solutions pave the way for sustainable growth and long-term success in today's competitive business environment.

In the realm of accounting, ensuring compliance with financial regulations is paramount to the success and reputation of any organization. To implement digital solutions that guarantee continual compliance, it is crucial to strategize effectively and integrate these solutions seamlessly into existing processes. **One key strategy** is to assess the current state of compliance within the organization thoroughly. By conducting a comprehensive audit of existing practices, potential gaps can be identified, and a roadmap for digital integration can be outlined.

Next, it is essential to involve key stakeholders in the decision-making process. Collaboration between finance, IT, and compliance departments can lead to a more holistic understanding of the organization's needs and challenges. By gathering insights from various perspectives, a tailored approach to implementing digital solutions can be crafted, ensuring buy-in from all relevant parties.

Another vital aspect is selecting the right digital tools for compliance. With a myriad of software options available in the market, it is crucial to choose solutions that align with the organization's specific requirements. Whether it's automated reporting systems, cloud-based storage for secure data management, or AI-driven analytics for real-time insights, selecting the most suitable tools can streamline compliance processes efficiently.

Moreover, training and upskilling employees on new digital tools are imperative for successful implementation. Resistance to change is common when introducing new technologies; therefore, providing comprehensive training programs can ease this transition and empower staff to utilize digital solutions effectively. Investing in employee development fosters a culture of continuous learning and adaptability within the organization.

Furthermore, establishing clear protocols and guidelines for using digital tools in compliance processes is essential. By creating standardized procedures for data input, analysis, and reporting, organizations can ensure consistency and accuracy in their compliance efforts. These protocols act as a roadmap for employees, guiding them through the intricacies of utilizing digital solutions for maintaining compliance.

Additionally, regular monitoring and evaluation of digital compliance processes are critical for ongoing success. By setting up mechanisms to track performance metrics, identify bottlenecks, and address any issues promptly, organizations can fine-tune their digital strategies continuously. This iterative approach allows for refinement and optimization of compliance procedures over time.

Lastly, fostering a culture of innovation and adaptability within the organization is key to sustaining compliance through digital solutions. Encouraging employees to embrace new technologies, share best practices, and provide feedback on existing processes cultivates an environment conducive to growth and improvement. By instilling a mindset of continuous improvement, organizations can stay ahead of regulatory changes and proactively address compliance challenges.

Incorporating these strategies into the implementation of digital solutions for compliance not only ensures adherence to financial regulations but also fosters efficiency, transparency, and accountability within the organization. By embracing technological advancements in accounting practices, organizations can navigate the complex landscape of compliance with confidence and resilience.

Navigating the intricate landscape of financial regulations without faltering is not just advisable; it's imperative for the longevity and credibility of any organization. The severe implications of non-compliance, ranging from hefty fines to irreparable reputational damage, underscore the critical nature of this endeavor. However, the journey toward compliance need not be a daunting voyage through uncharted waters. The advent of digital accounting technologies offers a beacon of hope, illuminating a path toward streamlined processes and reduced risks.

Digital accounting is not just a tool; it's a strategic ally in the quest for compliance. By automating routine tasks and ensuring accurate reporting, these technologies free up valuable resources, allowing firms to focus on strategic growth rather than getting bogged down by the fear of oversight. It's akin to having a vigilant guardian that never sleeps, constantly monitoring transactions to ensure they align with the latest regulatory standards.

But integrating digital solutions into existing frameworks is more than a mere technical upgrade; it's a transformative journey that requires thoughtful planning and execution. It demands an entrepreneurial spirit, willing to embrace innovation and navigate through temporary disruptions for a more compliant and efficient future. Remember, the objective is not just to survive but to thrive in an ever-evolving regulatory landscape.

Consider the stories of countless organizations that have turned potential adversity into opportunity by adopting digital accounting solutions. They didn't just avoid penalties; they unlocked new avenues for growth, enhanced their reputations, and built stronger relationships with stakeholders through transparent and reliable reporting.

So, as we reflect on the insights shared in this discourse, let us adopt a proactive stance towards compliance. **Let's view digital accounting not as an optional upgrade but as an essential cornerstone** of modern financial management. The journey may require patience and perseverance, but the rewards—safeguarding your organization's reputation and ensuring its sustainable growth—are well worth the effort.

In embracing these technologies and strategies, we're not just complying with regulations; we're setting new benchmarks for excellence in financial stewardship. Let this realization empower us to move forward with confidence, knowing that we possess the tools and knowledge to navigate the complexities of compliance with grace and efficiency.

Chapter 4: From History Books to Crystal Balls: The Proactive Power of Digital

The afternoon sun filtered through the blinds, casting long shadows across the cluttered desk where James sat, his eyes fixed on the screen, but his mind adrift in a sea of numbers that refused to make sense. The accounting software was outdated, a relic from an age when ledgers were king and digital was a foreign concept. He leaned back in his chair, the leather creaking under the weight of his frustration. The figures from last quarter loomed over him like specters of an ancient past, mocking him with their obsolescence.

Outside, the city hummed with life, a stark contrast to the stillness of James' office where time seemed to have stopped. He could hear faint laughter from the street below — people living in the moment while he was trapped in history's grasp. It was as if he was peering through a window into a world that had moved on without him.

James shook his head, trying to dispel the fog of doubt that clouded his thoughts. He knew there had to be a better way — something beyond this reactive stance that left him constantly playing catch-up with reality. He envisioned an oasis where data flowed like water from a spring, immediate and pure. A place where decisions could be made not just on what had been but what could be.

His colleague Maria passed by his door and offered a sympathetic smile before disappearing down the hall. She had mentioned something about automation once — how it had transformed her friend's business, made it more agile. The word echoed in James' mind: agile. It promised speed and adaptability; it whispered of freedom from mundane tasks that consumed so much of his precious time.

A gust of wind rattled the windowpane as if urging him to break free from these chains of inertia. Perhaps it was time to embrace this digital revolution fully, not just in bits and pieces as he had done before but wholly and completely. Could he become an architect of financial strategy rather than its janitor? Could he turn data into actionable insight with lightning speed?

He imagined himself at the helm of this new way forward — no longer sifting through piles of paper but navigating streams of live data that painted pictures clearer than any spreadsheet could hope to achieve. With each click, patterns would emerge; strategies would form in real-time.

The sun dipped lower now; its light grew softer but no less insistent as if highlighting the path he knew he must take. Tomorrow would be different; tomorrow he would begin anew.

In this quiet moment before dusk settled in fully, one question lingered in James' mind: How might embracing digital solutions not only change his approach but redefine his entire role within this relentless tide called progress?

Embrace the Future: Transform Your Accounting Practices Today

The accounting world is on the brink of a transformative shift, moving away from the historical and reactive nature of traditional practices towards a future where real-time data and proactive decision-making reign supreme. This evolution is not just a matter of adopting new technologies but represents a fundamental change in how businesses approach their financial management. The key to unlocking this potential lies in understanding the limitations of reactive, traditional accounting practices, appreciating the benefits of real-time data access and task automation, and exploring how digital accounting enables insightful, proactive decision-making.

Reactive accounting has long been the norm, with businesses looking backwards to understand their financial health. This approach, while familiar, is fraught with limitations. It often results in delayed responses to financial challenges and missed opportunities for growth because decisions are based on outdated information. Recognizing these limitations is the first step towards transformation. By acknowledging that past performance is not always a reliable indicator of future success, businesses can begin to see the value in a more forward-looking approach.

The advent of digital technologies in accounting has been nothing short of revolutionary. Real-time data access and task automation stand out as game-changers in this respect. These innovations allow businesses to monitor their financial health as it happens, providing an up-to-the-minute picture that can inform more timely and accurate decision-making. The efficiency gains from automating routine tasks cannot be overstated either; they free up valuable time for accountants to focus on strategic planning rather than getting bogged down in manual data entry or reconciliation tasks.

However, the true power of digital accounting lies in its ability to enable proactive, insightful decision-making. With advanced analytics tools, businesses can now sift through vast amounts of data to identify trends, forecast future performance, and make informed decisions that drive growth. This shift from reactive to proactive accounting is akin to moving from reading history books to gazing into crystal balls; it's about using insights gleaned from real-time data to shape a prosperous future rather than simply reacting to events after they've happened.

For those ready to embark on this journey, embracing digital solutions is key. But it's not just about adopting new software or platforms; it's about cultivating a mindset that values agility, foresight, and innovation. This chapter aims to guide you through this transformative process, offering practical tips and real-world examples that illustrate how embracing digital technologies can streamline operations, ensure compliance more effectively, and ultimately lead to smarter business decisions.

As we delve deeper into the specifics of transitioning from traditional to digital accounting practices, keep an open mind. Consider how these changes could apply within your own organization or practice. Reflect on the potential for not just surviving but thriving in an increasingly complex and fast-paced business environment. The journey ahead may seem daunting at first glance, but with the right tools and mindset, it's one that promises significant rewards for those willing to embrace change.

In navigating this digital shift, remember that you're not alone. The community of forward-thinking accountants and business owners embracing these changes is growing every day. By leaning into this network for support and guidance, you can overcome any hurdles along the way. Together, we can redefine what it means to be successful in accounting by turning insights into action and forging a path toward a more proactive and prosperous future.

Traditional accounting practices have long been the bedrock of financial management, relying on historical data and manual processes to track and analyze transactions. However, this reactive approach often leaves organizations playing catch-up, making decisions based on outdated information and facing challenges in forecasting future trends. The limitations of traditional accounting can hinder growth, create inefficiencies, and increase the risk of errors due to manual entry processes. In today's fast-paced business environment, where agility and real-time decision-making are paramount, the need for a shift towards proactive accounting practices has never been more pressing.

Real-time Data Access: One of the key drawbacks of traditional accounting is the lack of real-time data access. Waiting for monthly or quarterly reports means missed opportunities and potential risks going unnoticed until it's too late. With digital solutions, organizations can access up-to-the-minute financial information at their fingertips, allowing for quick responses to market changes and trends. This real-time data access empowers decision-makers to make informed choices promptly, driving growth and mitigating risks effectively.

Task Automation: Another limitation of traditional accounting is the heavy reliance on manual processes, leading to inefficiencies and increased chances of human error. By embracing digital tools for task automation, organizations can streamline repetitive tasks such as data entry, reconciliation, and reporting. Automation not only saves time but also improves accuracy by reducing the likelihood of human mistakes. This shift towards automation frees up valuable resources that can be redirected towards strategic initiatives rather than mundane administrative tasks.

Proactive Decision-Making: Perhaps the most significant benefit of transitioning from reactive to proactive accounting practices is the ability to make informed decisions based on valuable insights. Digital solutions offer advanced analytics and forecasting capabilities that enable organizations to anticipate trends, identify opportunities for growth, and proactively address potential challenges. By leveraging these insights, organizations can stay ahead of the curve, adapt quickly to changing market conditions, and drive innovation within their financial management processes.

In essence, understanding the limitations of reactive, traditional accounting practices is the first step towards embracing a more proactive approach that leverages digital solutions. Real-time data access, task automation, and proactive decision-making are key pillars in this transformative shift towards efficient financial management practices. By recognizing these limitations and embracing digital tools for innovation, organizations can unlock new levels of efficiency, accuracy, and strategic foresight in their accounting processes.

Dive deeper into how digital solutions can revolutionize your financial management practices...

In the realm of accounting, the ability to access real-time data and automate tasks marks a significant shift towards efficiency and accuracy. **Gone are the days of sifting through piles of paperwork and waiting for reports to be manually compiled**. With digital solutions at your fingertips, you can now **access up-to-the-minute financial information** that empowers you to make informed decisions swiftly. Imagine the power of having **instant insights into your organization's financial health**, allowing you to pivot strategies, seize opportunities, and address challenges with agility.

Task automation is another game-changer in the accounting landscape. By automating repetitive processes such as data entry, invoice generation, and reconciliation, you free up valuable time that can be redirected towards strategic thinking and analysis. No longer bogged down by mundane tasks, you can focus on **value-added activities** that drive growth and innovation within your organization. Embracing automation not only enhances productivity but also minimizes the risk of human error, ensuring **greater accuracy** in your financial records.

The beauty of real-time data access combined with task automation lies in their synergy. As you harness the power of digital tools to streamline your accounting processes, you pave the way for **proactive decision-making** based on accurate, current information. Picture yourself being able to **anticipate trends**, identify potential risks, and capitalize on emerging opportunities before they fully materialize. This proactive approach transforms you from a mere observer of past events to a visionary leader steering your organization towards success.

With digital advancements at your disposal, you hold the key to unlocking a new realm of possibilities in accounting. The ability to access real-time data and automate tasks not only boosts efficiency but also elevates the quality of your decision-making. By embracing these tools, you position yourself at the forefront of change, ready to navigate the complexities of today's dynamic business environment with confidence and clarity.

Framework Model: The Proactive Accounting Cycle

Real-time Data Collection

In this initial stage, businesses automate the collection of financial transactions as they occur, leveraging digital tools to ensure **timely and accurate** data. By capturing data in real-time, organizations lay a **solid foundation** for the subsequent stages of the accounting cycle. This step is critical in shifting from reactive to proactive accounting practices, enabling businesses to make decisions based on the most current information available.

Data Analysis and Interpretation

The second stage involves utilizing advanced analytics and artificial intelligence to interpret raw data, extracting **meaningful insights** about financial health, trends, and potential anomalies or fraud. Through **sophisticated algorithms**, businesses can uncover patterns and correlations that may not be immediately apparent, empowering them to make informed decisions based on a deeper understanding of their financial data.

Strategic Financial Planning

Building upon the insights gained from data analysis, the strategic financial planning stage focuses on using this information to forecast financial trajectories, plan budgets, and make informed decisions aligned with the organization's financial goals. By proactively utilizing data-driven strategies, businesses can **anticipate challenges**, seize opportunities, and optimize their financial performance for sustained success.

Real-time Reporting and Decision Making

In this stage, organizations leverage digital tools to disseminate insights and reports to relevant stakeholders almost instantaneously. This enables **agile decision-making processes**, allowing businesses to respond quickly to changing market conditions, regulatory requirements, or internal challenges. By streamlining communication and access to critical information, companies can enhance their ability to make timely and impactful decisions.

Continuous Feedback and Improvement

The final stage emphasizes the importance of learning from the outcomes of decisions made throughout the accounting cycle. By continuously gathering feedback and analyzing results, organizations can identify areas for improvement, refine strategies, and adjust tactics in an ongoing cycle of **continuous improvement**. This iterative process ensures that businesses remain adaptable, responsive, and forward-thinking in their financial management practices.

By following this proactive accounting cycle model, businesses can transition from reactive approaches reliant on historical data to a future-oriented stance driven by real-time insights and informed decision-making. The integration of digital technologies throughout the accounting process enables organizations to enhance efficiency, accuracy, and agility in managing their finances.

Practical Implications

The proactive accounting cycle model offers practical benefits for businesses seeking to optimize their financial management practices. By embracing real-time data collection, advanced analytics, strategic planning, rapid decision-making, and continuous improvement, organizations can unlock new opportunities for growth, mitigate risks proactively, and maintain a competitive edge in today's dynamic business environment.

Summary

The Proactive Accounting Cycle model represents a transformative shift towards proactive accounting practices enabled by digital technologies. By automating data collection processes, leveraging advanced analytics for interpretation, integrating insights into strategic planning, facilitating real-time reporting and decision-making, and embracing continuous feedback for improvement, businesses can revolutionize their approach to financial management. This framework underscores the importance of agility, adaptability, and foresight in navigating the complexities of modern finance.

The journey through the digital shift in accounting, as we have explored, is not merely about adopting new technologies. It's about fundamentally changing our mindset from a reactive to a proactive stance. This transformation is critical in today's fast-paced business environment, where relying on historical data and manual processes can no longer suffice. The limitations of traditional accounting practices are clear, and the path forward demands an embrace of digital solutions that offer real-time data access and task automation.

Embracing digital accounting is not just about efficiency; it's about the power it gives us to make informed decisions swiftly. Imagine having the ability to foresee challenges and opportunities, to strategize based on current data rather than past events. This is the promise of digital accounting—a promise that countless businesses and professionals have already begun to realize.

Reflect for a moment on your own practices. Have you ever felt constrained by the pace at which you can access or analyze financial information? Consider the transformative impact of having these insights at your fingertips, enabling you to act with confidence and foresight. This is not a distant dream but a very attainable reality with the tools and technologies available today.

Moreover, this shift towards proactive accounting practices fosters a culture of continuous improvement and innovation within organizations. It encourages us to ask better questions, to seek deeper insights, and to pursue excellence in every transaction and decision. *By making the leap into digital accounting*, we're not just keeping up with the times; we're setting ourselves up as leaders who shape the future of our industries.

Remember, every significant change begins with a single step. Whether you're a seasoned professional or just starting out, the journey towards proactive accounting is one that promises growth, resilience, and success in an ever-evolving digital landscape.

Let's take this step together—embracing the challenges, celebrating the victories, and always striving for greater understanding and insight. The power of proactive decision-making in accounting is immense, and by harnessing it, we unlock not just efficiency and compliance but also a world of potential for innovation and strategic success.

The transition from history books to crystal balls may seem daunting at first glance, but it's a journey well worth embarking on. With each step forward, we're not just adapting; we're transforming how we view and manage finances in a digital age—proactively shaping our future with clarity, confidence, and strategic insight.

Chapter 5: Growing Pains: Ensuring Your Accounting Solutions Scale with You

The early morning light spilled across the desk of Thomas Caldwell, a man whose life was as neatly ordered as the ledger books that lay open before him. His office, a quiet room adorned with the minimalistic charm of function over form, held the scent of freshly brewed coffee and the faint hum of a city awakening. Today's agenda: to confront the growing pains of his burgeoning enterprise.

As he sipped his coffee, Thomas let his mind drift to yesterday's board meeting, where words like "scalability" and "digital transformation" bounced off the walls like echoes in an empty hall. The company had outgrown its humble beginnings; transactions now numbered in thousands where they once trickled in by tens and twenties.

He recalled his father's small business, how it had remained confined within the walls of limited technology and foresight. A pang of nostalgia touched him briefly before determination set its jaws into his plans for expansion. He would not allow history to repeat itself under his watch.

The chime of an incoming email pulled Thomas back from reverie to reality. It was a proposal from yet another software vendor promising seamless integration and unlimited scalability. He leaned back in his chair, fingers steepled against his lips. Could this be the solution? Or just another hopeful shot in the dark?

The decision weighed on him like anchors on a ship set to sail uncharted waters. He needed a digital accounting solution that would not only support current operations but also anticipate future growth – one that could evolve as swiftly as market demands dictated.

A colleague stepped into the office, breaking through his contemplation with a simple inquiry about weekend plans. Thomas smiled faintly, giving nothing away of the turmoil inside as he returned pleasantries. Once alone again, he turned to gaze out at the skyline that seemed to stretch endlessly just like the potential of his company.

Would he find a system robust enough to withstand rapid growth without buckling under pressure? Could there be an unseen flaw in these digital promises waiting to unravel at a moment's notice?

In moments such as these where past experiences and future aspirations collided with present decisions, one could not help but wonder: How does one measure certainty against ambition when charting unknown territories?

The Scale of Success: Growing Your Business Without Outgrowing Your Accounting Software

In the dynamic landscape of modern business, the ability to adapt and grow is not just an advantage—it's a necessity. This truth extends beyond product lines, market strategies, and even personnel to the very core of operational systems, particularly accounting. As businesses evolve, the demand for digital accounting solutions that can not only keep pace but also enhance this growth becomes increasingly critical. The big idea here is straightforward yet profound: **Scalability in digital accounting solutions is non-negotiable**. It's about choosing software that grows with your business, accommodating increasing transaction volumes and adapting to changing requirements with grace and efficiency.

Identifying essential features for scalable digital accounting solutions is the first step on this journey. It involves understanding what scalability truly means in the context of digital accounting—whether it's cloud-based adaptability, real-time data processing capabilities, or seamless integration with other business systems. These features ensure that as your business expands, your accounting software can effortlessly match its pace without necessitating frequent upgrades or system overhauls.

Understanding the implications of scalability for long-term business growth goes hand in hand with recognizing these essential features. A scalable digital accounting solution does more than just record transactions; it provides actionable insights that help drive strategic decisions. It's about turning data into a competitive edge that not only illuminates past performance but also forecasts future trends.

Selecting software that evolves with your business needs might seem daunting at first glance. Yet, it's entirely feasible with a strategic approach that prioritizes flexibility, customizability, and support. This means opting for solutions that offer extensive customization options to meet unique business needs and choosing providers known for their robust customer support and commitment to continuous improvement.

Through personal anecdotes and examples of businesses that have successfully navigated these waters, this chapter aims to inspire confidence in the selection process. It's filled with stories of entrepreneurs who faced the challenge of scaling their accounting systems head-on, turning potential obstacles into stepping stones towards greater efficiency and success.

Encouraging reflection and introspection among readers is crucial. Consider your current system's limitations: Can it handle a significant increase in transaction volume? Does it integrate seamlessly with other tools you might need as you grow? If not, what steps can you take today to start moving towards a more scalable solution?

This journey towards scalable digital accounting solutions isn't just about ensuring your software can keep up with your business growth—it's about future-proofing your financial systems to unlock efficiency and compliance with ease. It represents a strategic investment in your company's future—one that pays dividends by enabling focus on expansion and innovation rather than wrestling with outdated systems.

By embracing scalable digital accounting solutions, businesses can navigate the challenges of growth without fear of outpacing their infrastructure. This chapter serves as both a roadmap and a beacon for those ready to ensure their accounting practices are as dynamic and adaptable as their ambitions.

Scalability is a critical consideration when selecting digital accounting solutions for your business. As your company grows, so will the volume of transactions, data, and reporting requirements. Therefore, it is essential to identify the key features that will enable your accounting system to expand seamlessly alongside your business.

One crucial aspect to look for in scalable digital accounting solutions is flexibility. The software should be able to adapt to changing business needs, whether it's accommodating new revenue streams, handling increased transaction volumes, or adjusting to regulatory changes. A rigid system can quickly become a bottleneck as your business evolves, leading to inefficiencies and potential errors.

Another essential feature of scalable accounting solutions is integration capabilities. The software should be able to connect with other tools and systems used in your organization, such as CRM software, inventory management systems, or payment processors. Seamless integration streamlines data flow across different departments and reduces manual data entry, saving time and minimizing errors.

Automation is a key component of scalability. Look for accounting solutions that offer automation features for routine tasks like invoice processing, expense tracking, and reconciliation. Automating these processes not only improves efficiency but also reduces the risk of human error as your business grows.

Scalable digital accounting solutions should also prioritize data security. With the increasing volume of financial data being processed, stored, and transmitted, robust security measures are essential to protect sensitive information from cyber threats. Look for software that offers encryption, access controls, regular security updates, and compliance with industry standards.

Real-time reporting and analytics capabilities are crucial for scalability. As your business expands, you need timely insights into your financial performance to make informed decisions. The ability to generate customizable reports, track key performance indicators (KPIs), and analyze trends in real-time can help you stay agile and responsive in a dynamic business environment.

Are you ready to unlock the full potential of scalable digital accounting solutions? Let's explore how these features can revolutionize your accounting processes and pave the way for sustainable growth in your business...

Scalability is not just a buzzword; it's a critical factor that can determine the success or failure of your business in the long run. As your company grows, so do your accounting needs. Understanding the implications of scalability for long-term business growth is essential to avoid hitting roadblocks that could hinder your progress. **Investing in digital accounting solutions that can scale with your business is an investment in your future success.**

When considering scalability, think about the trajectory of your business. Are you planning to expand into new markets? Will you be handling more transactions in the future? **Scalable accounting solutions should not only meet your current needs but also have the capacity to adapt to increased demand and changing requirements.** Imagine a scenario where your business experiences rapid growth, but your accounting software struggles to keep up, leading to delays, errors, and inefficiencies. By choosing scalable solutions from the outset, you can avoid these pitfalls and ensure smooth operations as you expand.

One common misconception is that scalability is only a concern for large corporations. However, businesses of all sizes can benefit from scalable accounting solutions. Whether you're a small startup with ambitious growth plans or an established company looking to streamline operations, scalability is key to maintaining efficiency and competitiveness in today's fast-paced business landscape. **By investing in scalable digital accounting solutions early on, you set a strong foundation for sustainable growth and success.**

The beauty of scalable accounting solutions lies in their ability to grow alongside your business organically. Instead of constantly outgrowing your software and having to switch platforms, **scalable solutions offer flexibility and adaptability,** saving you time and resources in the long term. Picture a scenario where every time your business expands, you need to undergo a complex and costly migration process to upgrade your accounting software. This not only disrupts your operations but also introduces risks and uncertainties into your financial processes.

Embracing scalability means future-proofing your business against unforeseen challenges and opportunities. It means having the agility to pivot when necessary without being held back by outdated systems or limited capabilities. **By understanding the implications of scalability for long-term business growth,** you position yourself for sustainable success in an ever-evolving market landscape.

In conclusion, scalability is not just about accommodating growth; it's about setting yourself up for long-term prosperity by making strategic decisions today that will benefit your business tomorrow. **Choose scalable digital accounting solutions wisely, and watch as your business flourishes with ease and efficiency**—empowering you to focus on what truly matters: driving innovation, serving customers better, and achieving your vision for the future.

In selecting software that evolves with your business needs, it's crucial to consider not just the current state of your operations but also the potential growth and changes your business may undergo in the future. **Scalability** is key here; you want a solution that can flex and adapt as your organization expands. Look for platforms that offer **customization** options, allowing you to tailor the software to suit your specific requirements.

When assessing accounting software, **integration capabilities** are paramount. Your chosen system should be able to seamlessly connect with other tools and applications you use in your business. This integration ensures smooth data flow and eliminates the need for manual data entry, reducing errors and saving time.

Another essential factor to consider is **cloud-based solutions**. Cloud accounting software provides the flexibility to access your financial data from anywhere, at any time. This accessibility becomes increasingly important as businesses grow and expand geographically or adopt remote work setups.

Automation is a game-changer when it comes to evolving software solutions. By automating repetitive tasks such as data entry, invoicing, and reconciliation, you can free up valuable time for more strategic financial activities. Additionally, automation reduces the risk of human error, enhancing the accuracy of your financial records.

As your business grows, **reporting capabilities** become increasingly important. The ability to generate detailed reports quickly and accurately is vital for making informed decisions based on real-time data. Ensure that the software you choose offers robust reporting features that align with your business needs.

Consider the **support and training** provided by the software vendor. As your business evolves, you may need additional assistance or guidance on using advanced features. Opt for a vendor that offers comprehensive support options and training resources to help you make the most of your accounting software.

Lastly, keep an eye on **updates and upgrades**. A good software provider will regularly release updates to improve functionality, security, and performance. Make sure you choose a solution that is regularly maintained and updated to stay ahead of technological advancements and changing business requirements.

By selecting accounting software that can evolve with your business needs, you set yourself up for long-term success and efficiency. Embrace scalability, integration, automation, cloud capabilities, robust reporting features, support services, and ongoing updates to ensure that your accounting solution grows alongside your business.

Navigating the digital transformation in accounting is akin to setting sail into uncharted waters. The choices made at the onset, particularly concerning scalable digital accounting solutions, will determine the smoothness of your journey and the success of your venture. Recognizing that scalability is not merely a feature but a foundation for future growth is crucial. **It ensures that as your business expands, your accounting system evolves in tandem, without missing a beat.**

Imagine a scenario where you're scaling new heights in your business. The volume of transactions multiplies, and suddenly, the accounting software that once seemed infallible begins to falter. This is a common pitfall many encounter, yet it is entirely avoidable. The key lies in selecting software that not only meets current needs but anticipates future demands. *It's about making an informed choice today that continues to pay dividends tomorrow.*

Reflect for a moment on the implications of scalability for long-term growth. A scalable solution does more than keep pace with your expanding business—it propels it forward. By ensuring efficiency and compliance are maintained regardless of scale, it enables you to focus on strategic growth areas with confidence. Think of it as having a trusted partner by your side, one that's equipped to handle whatever the future holds.

Selecting the right software requires introspection and foresight. Consider where you see your business in five, ten, or even twenty years.

Will the solution you choose today be able to support that vision? This question isn't just rhetorical; it's a critical consideration for ensuring long-term success.

Let's draw inspiration from those who have traversed this path successfully. Entrepreneurs who embraced scalable solutions from the outset have shared how this decision allowed them to navigate growth with agility and assurance. Their stories underscore the transformative power of strategic foresight in digital accounting solutions.

In essence, ensuring your accounting solutions scale with you is about **embracing change with open arms**. It's about recognizing that what works today may not suffice tomorrow and acting proactively to address this reality. By identifying essential features for scalability, understanding its implications for growth, and discovering how to select software that evolves with your business needs, you're not just preparing for the future—you're shaping it.

As we move forward, let this chapter serve as both a guide and a reminder of the importance of scalability in digital accounting solutions. It's an investment in your business's future and a commitment to sustained success. With strategic thinking, innovation, and an eye towards long-term efficiency and effectiveness, you're well-equipped to navigate the digital shift in accounting with confidence and ease.

Let us carry forward this entrepreneurial spirit and strategic foresight into every aspect of our businesses. By doing so, we ensure not only our own success but also contribute to a more efficient, compliant, and robust digital accounting landscape for all.

Chapter 6: Technological Fluency: Mastering the Tools of Digital Accounting

The sun hung high over the skyline, its rays casting long shadows through the glass-paneled office where Martin sat surrounded by mountains of paper and the soft hum of a computer. The room smelled faintly of ink and the promise of rain from the heavy clouds gathering outside. He had been an accountant for years, steadfast in his ways, but now the ground beneath him was shifting.

He remembered the days when ledgers were his scripture and a pen was his faithful companion. But whispers of change rustled through the financial world like wind through autumn leaves – cloud-based accounting software was no longer just a whisper; it was a shout that echoed in every corner of his profession.

Martin's fingers paused above his keyboard, lingering with hesitation. He had seen how automation transformed tedious tasks into mere afterthoughts for those who embraced it. Customized reporting had turned raw data into clear insights for others, insights that he grappled to glean from endless columns of numbers.

The phone rang, jarring him from his thoughts. It was another client asking for real-time financial analysis, something Martin knew he couldn't provide with his current tools. His chest tightened with a mix of fear and resolve; he knew he must adapt or risk becoming obsolete in this digital age.

Later that afternoon, as he watched younger colleagues effortlessly navigate various software platforms, integrating them like maestros conducting an orchestra, a realization dawned on him. His dedication to continuous learning had been unwavering once; it was time to rekindle that flame.

As dusk approached and the office emptied, Martin sat alone with only the glow of his screen for company. He pondered over courses and tutorials on digital accounting tools – they were keys to unlock efficiency and productivity he had never known before.

There was comfort in knowing that even as technology advanced at breakneck speed, human curiosity and adaptability marched alongside it. And so as night fell over the cityscape and lights flickered on one by one, Martin found himself at a crossroads between tradition and innovation.

Will this journey into digital mastery reforge him into an indispensable asset or will it be a path littered with more challenges than triumphs?

Harnessing the Power of Digital Tools in Accounting

In an era where technology evolves at a breakneck speed, mastering digital tools has become not just an advantage but a necessity for accounting professionals. The leap from traditional ledger-based accounting to digital platforms may seem daunting, yet it paves the way for unparalleled efficiency, accuracy, and strategic decision-making. This journey towards technological fluency in digital accounting is not merely about adopting new software; it's about embracing a culture of continuous learning and innovation.

The core of this transformation lies in understanding and leveraging cloud-based accounting software. These platforms offer more than just convenience; they are a gateway to real-time financial data, insightful analytics, and streamlined processes that were once unimaginable. **Cloud-based solutions** democratize access to powerful accounting tools, making them available anywhere, at any time. This shift not only enhances productivity but also fosters a more collaborative work environment.

However, the transition to digital accounting is not without its challenges. Acquiring skills in **automation, customized reporting,**

and software integration demands a proactive approach to learning. It's about diving deep into the functionalities of the software, understanding its capabilities, and tailoring it to fit the unique needs of your business. This process involves not just individual effort but also nurturing a team culture that values upskilling and technological adaptability.

A Step-by-Step Guide to Embracing Digital Accounting Tools

Step 1: Understand the core functionalities of cloud-based accounting software

The first step in this journey is to research and identify reputable cloud-based accounting software providers. Comparing features, scalability, and compatibility with your business needs is crucial. Engage with free trials or demonstrations to see these platforms in action. This exploration phase is foundational, setting the stage for informed decision-making.

Step 2: Acquire skills in automation, customized reporting, and software integration

Once you've selected a platform, dive into its specifics through training sessions or webinars provided by the software provider. Online tutorials and resources can be invaluable for learning the ins and outs of the software. Practice with sample data to build confidence and explore customization options to meet your reporting needs fully. Integrating other systems like CRM or inventory management tools can further streamline your processes.

Step 3: Emphasize the importance of continuous technology

learning for optimizing accounting practices

Fostering a culture of curiosity within your team is pivotal. Encourage participation in ongoing training and provide resources for keeping abreast of technological advancements. Sharing success stories can inspire others and demonstrate tangible benefits of embracing digital tools.

This process isn't just about technical mastery; it's about cultivating an attitude of openness towards innovation. Success lies not just in implementing new tools but in continuously evaluating their impact on your practices and looking for ways to optimize them further.

The transition to digital accounting represents a significant shift in how professionals approach their work—moving from manual calculations and reactive decision-making to proactive strategic planning enabled by real-time data analysis. As daunting as this journey might seem at first glance, remember that every step taken towards mastering these digital tools brings you closer to achieving unprecedented levels of efficiency and insight in your accounting practices.

Embracing this change requires patience, dedication, and a willingness to experiment. But the rewards—increased productivity, better decision-making capabilities, and enhanced competitive advantage—are well worth the effort. Let's embark on this journey together, transforming challenges into opportunities for growth and innovation in the digital age.

Cloud-based accounting software is not just a tool; it's a game-changer for modern accounting practices. By mastering the core functionalities and benefits of these digital platforms, accounting professionals can revolutionize their workflow, enhance accuracy, and improve decision-making processes. One of the key advantages of cloud-based accounting software is its accessibility - allowing users to access financial data anytime, anywhere, with just an internet connection. This convenience empowers accountants to work remotely, collaborate seamlessly with team members, and stay on top of financial tasks efficiently.

Another significant benefit of cloud-based accounting software is its automation capabilities. Tasks that were once manual and time-consuming can now be automated, freeing up valuable time for accountants to focus on higher-value activities. From invoice processing to expense tracking, automation reduces human error and increases efficiency. Moreover, customizable reporting features enable users to generate insightful financial reports tailored to specific business needs. These reports provide a comprehensive overview of the company's financial health, facilitating informed decision-making and strategic planning.

Additionally, cloud-based accounting software offers seamless integration with a variety of third-party applications, expanding its functionality and versatility. Integrating with other tools such as payment gateways or CRM systems enhances the software's capabilities, streamlines processes, and ensures data consistency across platforms. This interoperability is essential for creating a connected ecosystem that optimizes efficiency and productivity in accounting operations.

Ready to delve deeper into the world of cloud-based accounting software?

Mastering these tools is not just about staying current; it's about transforming your accounting practices for the better. Join us as we explore automation features, customized reporting options, and the power of software integration in the next section.

In the realm of digital accounting, acquiring proficiency in automation, customized reporting, and software integration is paramount. These skills not only streamline processes but also enhance accuracy and decision-making capabilities. **Automation** stands as a cornerstone of efficiency in modern accounting practices. By automating routine tasks such as data entry, invoicing, and reconciliation, professionals can free up valuable time to focus on strategic analysis and planning. Embracing automation tools can significantly reduce errors and increase productivity, leading to a more agile and responsive financial operation.

Customized reporting plays a pivotal role in translating raw data into actionable insights. Tailoring reports to specific needs and key performance indicators allows for a more nuanced understanding of financial performance. By customizing reports to highlight critical metrics, accounting professionals can drive informed decision-making and strategic planning. Moreover, personalized reports cater to the diverse informational needs of stakeholders, fostering transparency and accountability within the organization.

Software integration represents the synergy between different tools and platforms to create a seamless ecosystem for accounting operations. Integrating various software applications enables data flow between systems, eliminating manual data entry errors and redundancies. This interconnected approach enhances data visibility and accessibility, empowering accounting teams to work collaboratively and efficiently across departments. By leveraging integrated software solutions, organizations can achieve greater operational agility and responsiveness in an ever-evolving business landscape.

Mastering these essential skills in automation, customized reporting, and software integration is crucial for staying competitive in the digital age of accounting. Embracing technological advancements not only streamlines processes but also unlocks new possibilities for growth and innovation within organizations. As accounting professionals navigate the complexities of digital tools, continuous learning and adaptation become fundamental pillars of success in optimizing financial operations.

Incorporating automation, customized reporting, and software integration into daily practices empowers accounting professionals to transcend traditional boundaries of efficiency and accuracy. By harnessing the full potential of digital tools, individuals can revolutionize their approach to financial management, driving sustainable growth and profitability. Through a commitment to ongoing learning and mastery of technology, accounting professionals can unlock the transformative power of digital tools to elevate their practice to new heights of success.

Analytical Framework: The Path to Digital Accounting Mastery

In the journey towards mastering digital accounting tools, a structured approach is crucial. This analytical framework consists of several interconnected layers, each playing a vital role in optimizing accounting practices and leveraging technology effectively. Let's delve into each layer to understand its significance and contribution to the overall model.

Technological Proficiency

Technological proficiency serves as the foundation of the framework, emphasizing the need for accountants to understand the functionalities of various software, particularly cloud-based solutions and automation tools. This layer equips professionals with the knowledge required to navigate modern accounting platforms efficiently. Without a solid grasp of these technologies, it becomes challenging to harness their full potential for enhancing productivity and decision-making processes.

Integration Capabilities

The **integration capabilities** layer focuses on how software can seamlessly integrate with existing systems. This aspect is essential for optimizing workflows, ensuring data consistency across platforms, and streamlining processes. By integrating different tools effectively, accountants can eliminate silos of information and create a more cohesive and interconnected accounting ecosystem.

Customization and Scalability

Customization and scalability highlight the importance of tailoring solutions to meet specific business needs while allowing room for growth. Customization enables organizations to adapt software functionalities to their unique requirements, enhancing efficiency and effectiveness. Scalability ensures that as businesses evolve, their accounting tools can grow with them, accommodating increased data volume and complexity.

Data Analysis and Reporting

The **data analysis and reporting** layer underscores the significance of tools that offer insightful analytics, customized reporting options, and real-time access to financial data. These capabilities empower accountants to make data-driven decisions, identify trends, and forecast future outcomes accurately. Access to comprehensive reporting features enables a deeper understanding of financial performance and aids in strategic planning.

Security and Compliance

The final layer of the framework is **security and compliance**, which ensures that selected tools not only protect sensitive financial data but also adhere to relevant regulations. Maintaining data security is paramount in the digital age where cybersecurity threats are prevalent.

Additionally, compliance with industry standards and regulations safeguards organizations from legal repercussions and instills trust among stakeholders.

This analytical framework provides a structured roadmap for accountants seeking to optimize their practices through technology mastery. By carefully considering each layer's role and interconnectivity within the model, professionals can navigate the complexities of digital accounting with confidence and efficiency.

Navigating the realm of digital accounting requires more than just a surface-level understanding of its tools and functionalities. It demands a deep dive into the core benefits of cloud-based software, an adeptness in leveraging automation, and a finesse in crafting customized reports and integrating diverse software solutions. Such skills are not just advantageous; they are **essential** for any accounting professional striving to enhance efficiency, productivity, and decision-making processes in today's fast-paced digital environment.

Imagine the possibilities when every number in your ledger not only tells a story but also provides actionable insights thanks to your mastery over these digital tools. Stories of businesses that turned their fortunes around by harnessing the power of automated reporting and integrated software systems are not just motivational anecdotes; they are testament to what can be achieved with the right skills and knowledge. These triumphs over adversity underscore the transformative power of technological fluency in accounting.

However, the journey doesn't end with acquiring these skills. The landscape of digital accounting is ever-evolving, with new technologies emerging at a rapid pace. This reality brings forth an important question: Are you committed to continuous learning to stay ahead of the curve? Embracing this commitment means opening doors to unprecedented levels of efficiency and strategic insight within your practice or business.

Remember, every step taken towards mastering these digital tools is a step towards unlocking your full potential as an accounting professional. It's about more than just keeping up; it's about leading the charge in innovation and strategic thinking. By prioritizing clarity, simplicity, and continuous learning, you not only become more proficient but also more valuable in this digital age.

So, let's not view technological fluency as a daunting challenge but as an exciting opportunity to grow and innovate. As we move forward, let's carry with us the entrepreneurial spirit that thrives on hard work, strategic thinking, and innovation. Let this chapter serve as a foundation upon which we build our journey towards excellence in digital accounting—a journey marked by efficiency, compliance, and above all, a relentless pursuit of knowledge.

The essence of mastering digital accounting tools lies not just in understanding their functionalities but in leveraging them to create real value for businesses and clients alike. As we continue navigating this digital shift, let us do so with confidence, knowing that our commitment to continuous learning and mastery of technology will undoubtedly lead us to success.

Chapter 7: The Vault: Safeguarding Your Financial Data in the Digital Age

The sun had begun its descent, casting long shadows across the small, cluttered office where Martin sat surrounded by piles of financial reports and glowing screens. It was a quiet evening, the kind that made the hum of the computer seem like the roar of an engine in an otherwise silent world. Martin's fingers danced across the keyboard with a weary expertise, navigating through spreadsheets that held numbers as vast as stars in the sky.

He paused, leaning back in his chair with a creak that spoke of too many hours spent in that very position. The weight of responsibility pressed down on him like the heavy air before a storm. His company had grown quickly, a testament to his hard work and vision, but with growth came complexity and risk. He knew it was time to transition to more secure accounting software; thoughts of data breaches and compliance nightmares had been gnawing at him for weeks.

In his mind's eye, he saw himself standing at a crossroads—one path leading towards secure fortresses of digital information, guarded by encrypted walls and vigilant sentinels; the other meandering into a murky forest where shadows whispered of audits and fraud. The choice seemed obvious, yet daunting all the same.

A gust of wind rattled the windowpane, drawing Martin's attention away from his reverie. Outside, people hurried along sidewalks beneath amber streetlights, their faces etched with concerns unknown to him but no less pressing than his own. He turned back to his computer screen where an open tab displayed reviews for various accounting software options—each promising compliance and iron-clad security.

Martin thought about his team; they were good people who cared about their work but were not experts in cybersecurity or regulatory intricacies. How would he foster an environment where best practices for digital security became second nature? The task seemed as delicate as weaving silk—a process both intricate and prone to unraveling if not handled with care.

A soft chime signaled an incoming email breaking into his contemplation—a reminder from IT about scheduled software updates. It was a start but only one piece of the larger puzzle he needed to solve. Updates were routine maintenance; what he sought was transformational change—a paradigm shift within his company's culture regarding data security.

He envisioned training sessions filled with eager faces hungry for knowledge on how to protect their digital domain—their shared kingdom where numbers ruled supreme and vigilance was now demanded by subjects unseen yet ever-present.

As twilight deepened into night outside his office window, Martin considered how education on these matters was much like lighting candles in darkness—it took just one spark to illuminate even the blackest night. But how many candles would it take before every corner was bathed in light?

His gaze fell once more upon those glowing screens—portals to infinite possibilities yet also potential gateways for those with malice in their hearts. Would he be able to lead his team into this new era securely? Could they adapt swiftly enough?

The moon rose high above as Martin closed down his computer for the night; its pale glow through blinds drew patterns on walls that seemed suddenly too fragile against what lay beyond them. What steps must one take when securing not just data but futures?

Your Financial Fortress: Building Security in a Digital World

In an era where digital transformation has permeated every facet of the business world, the safeguarding of financial data emerges as a paramount concern. The digital shift in accounting, a crucial aspect of this transformation, brings with it a host of benefits including efficiency and compliance. However, it also presents significant risks to data security. **Understanding the importance of selecting secure, compliant accounting software** is not just a recommendation; it's a necessity for businesses aiming to protect their financial data from cyber threats and regulatory penalties.

The journey towards securing your financial data in the digital age begins with a conscious effort to **research and select accounting software** that does not compromise on data security and compliance. This involves looking for certifications or industry endorsements that serve as a testament to the software's robust security measures. It is equally important to review the software's privacy policy and terms of service to ensure alignment with your organization's data protection standards. Direct engagement with software providers about their security protocols can offer deeper insights into how well your financial data will be protected.

Maintaining a secure digital accounting environment extends beyond the initial selection of software. It encompasses **best practices** such as implementing strong password policies, ensuring regular updates of all software and systems with the latest security patches, and backing up financial data in secure locations. Monitoring user activity within the accounting software is crucial for detecting unauthorized access. Moreover, educating your accounting staff about data security's importance cannot be overstressed. Regular training on best practices forms the backbone of a proactive defense against potential breaches.

Exploring strategies for **regular software updates** and team education on data security is another pillar supporting your financial fortress. Creating a schedule for regular updates ensures that your systems are always equipped with the latest defenses against cyber threats. Emphasizing to your team the critical role they play in maintaining this secure environment through continuous education on best practices is essential. Topics such as phishing awareness and safe browsing habits should be staples in this educational endeavor.

The Blueprint for Digital Defense

Step 1: Selecting Your Shield

- Dedicate time to thoroughly research potential accounting software, prioritizing those known for their strong stance on data security and compliance.

- Validate the software's credibility through certifications or industry endorsements.

- Ensure alignment with your organization's standards by reviewing privacy policies and directly discussing security protocols with providers.

Step 2: Fortifying Your Walls

- Enforce strong password policies across your team.

- Stay vigilant by applying the latest security patches without delay.

- Implement routine backups and monitor user activities to swiftly identify any discrepancies.

- Cultivate a culture of security awareness among staff through ongoing training.

Step 3: Keeping The Guard Up

- Establish a calendar for regular software updates, marking it as non-negotiable in your operational protocols.

- Foster an environment where updates are seen as vital to safeguarding your fortress, encouraging staff participation.

- Engage your team in continuous learning opportunities focused on emerging threats and defensive best practices.

The goal here is clear: transform your organization into an impenetrable fortress against cyber threats while ensuring compliance with regulatory standards. This process is not static; it requires adaptability, vigilance, and an unwavering commitment from every member of your team. Success looks like a seamlessly secure digital accounting environment where financial data remains protected against all odds.

Remember, building your financial fortress in the digital world doesn't happen overnight. It is an ongoing journey marked by strategic decisions, continuous learning, and relentless pursuit of excellence in data security practices. Engaging in this process wholeheartedly not only safeguards your organization's most sensitive information but also positions you as a leader in digital accountability and trustworthiness.

In the fast-paced digital age, safeguarding your financial data is paramount. Selecting accounting software from reputable vendors with robust security measures and compliance certifications is crucial. **Ensuring the protection of sensitive financial information** is not only a matter of organizational integrity but also a legal requirement in many industries. By choosing software that prioritizes security and compliance, you can mitigate risks and instill confidence in your stakeholders.

Regular software updates play a pivotal role in maintaining a secure accounting environment. These updates often include patches for any vulnerabilities that hackers could exploit. Ignoring updates could leave your system exposed to potential breaches. Furthermore, educating your staff on data security best practices is essential. **Empowering your team with knowledge** on how to recognize and respond to security threats can significantly enhance your overall defense against cyber attacks.

The digital transformation of accounting processes necessitates a proactive approach to data security. By investing in secure software solutions, you demonstrate your commitment to protecting sensitive information. **Compliance certifications**, such as SOC 1 and SOC 2, provide third-party validation of a software provider's adherence to stringent security standards. Prioritizing these certifications when selecting accounting software can offer peace of mind and ensure regulatory compliance.

As technology continues to evolve, so do the tactics of cybercriminals. Staying ahead of potential threats requires vigilance and a willingness to adapt. **Choosing software that offers multi-factor authentication** and encryption capabilities can add layers of security to your financial data. Additionally, implementing regular security audits can help identify vulnerabilities before they are exploited.

The path to a secure financial future begins with informed decisions.

By understanding the importance of selecting secure, compliant accounting software, you lay a strong foundation for protecting your organization's valuable data assets. In the digital age, where information is both powerful and vulnerable, making wise choices about your software solutions is key to safeguarding against cyber threats and ensuring regulatory adherence. Join us as we delve deeper into best practices for maintaining a secure digital accounting environment and explore strategies for continuous improvement in data security.

In the digital age, maintaining a secure environment for your financial data is paramount. **Best practices** must be implemented to safeguard sensitive information and ensure compliance with regulatory standards. One key aspect of maintaining a secure digital accounting environment is **choosing reputable software** that prioritizes security measures and holds compliance certifications. By selecting accounting software from trusted vendors, you can significantly reduce the risk of data breaches and ensure that your financial information remains protected.

Regular **software updates** play a crucial role in maintaining a secure digital accounting environment. These updates often include patches for security vulnerabilities, ensuring that your system is equipped with the latest defenses against potential threats. Ignoring software updates can leave your system vulnerable to cyber attacks, putting your financial data at risk. Therefore, it is essential to prioritize regular updates to enhance the security of your accounting software.

Aside from software updates, **staff education** on data security best practices is vital for maintaining a secure digital accounting environment. Training your team on how to identify phishing attempts, create strong passwords, and recognize potential security risks can significantly reduce the likelihood of a data breach. Educating your staff creates a culture of awareness and responsibility when it comes to data security, making them active participants in safeguarding sensitive financial information.

Implementing access controls within your accounting software is another best practice for maintaining a secure digital environment. By restricting access to sensitive financial data based on job roles and responsibilities, you can minimize the risk of unauthorized users gaining entry to critical information. Access controls ensure that only authorized personnel can view and manipulate sensitive financial data, adding an extra layer of security to your accounting processes.

Furthermore, **regular security audits** are essential for assessing the effectiveness of your security measures and identifying any potential vulnerabilities in your system. Conducting routine audits allows you to stay proactive in addressing security concerns and implementing necessary changes to fortify your digital accounting environment. By regularly evaluating your security protocols, you can continuously improve the protection of your financial data and adapt to evolving cybersecurity threats.

In conclusion, maintaining a secure digital accounting environment requires a multi-faceted approach that includes selecting reputable software, prioritizing regular updates, educating staff on data security best practices, implementing access controls, and conducting regular security audits. By following these best practices diligently, you can strengthen the security of your financial data, reduce the risk of cyber threats, and ensure compliance with regulatory standards in the digital age.

Now that you have selected secure accounting software and learned best practices for maintaining a safe digital accounting environment, it's crucial to explore strategies for **regular software updates** and **team education on data security**.

Regular software updates are essential to ensure that your accounting system remains protected against evolving cybersecurity threats. By staying current with the latest updates from your software provider, you can patch vulnerabilities and enhance the overall security of your financial data. Make it a priority to schedule routine checks for updates and implement them promptly to mitigate any potential risks to your system.

In addition to software updates, **team education on data security** is paramount in creating a culture of awareness within your organization. Conduct regular training sessions to educate your staff on the importance of data security, common cyber threats, and best practices for safeguarding sensitive information. Empower your team to recognize phishing attempts, use strong passwords, and follow established protocols for handling financial data securely.

Encouraging a mindset of continuous learning and improvement within your team can significantly strengthen your organization's defense against cyber threats. Consider implementing simulated phishing exercises to test your staff's response to potential threats and provide ongoing support and resources to help them stay informed about the latest cybersecurity trends.

By prioritizing **regular software updates** and **team education on data security**, you are taking proactive steps to fortify your accounting system against malicious attacks and ensuring the integrity of your financial data. Remember, cybersecurity is a shared responsibility that requires vigilance, collaboration, and a commitment to staying one step ahead of cybercriminals.

Navigating the digital shift in accounting is akin to embarking on an uncharted journey through a vast, evolving landscape. At the heart of this expedition lies the imperative to fortify our financial data against the relentless threats that pervade the digital realm. The essence of safeguarding our accounting practices, as we've discovered, hinges on a triad of critical strategies: selecting secure and compliant software, embedding best practices into our daily operations, and committing to continuous education and system updates.

Selecting the right accounting software is not merely a technical decision; it's a foundational investment in your company's integrity and future. Imagine a scenario where due to a hasty or uninformed choice, your organization's sensitive financial data becomes compromised. This isn't just about numbers; it's about people's livelihoods, trust, and the reputation painstakingly built over years. By prioritizing software that meets rigorous security standards and compliance certifications, we shield not only our data but also fortify the trust our clients place in us.

Maintaining a **secure digital accounting environment** transcends mere compliance. It reflects a commitment to excellence and a respect for the trust stakeholders place in our capabilities. Consider the tale of a small business that thrived despite industry giants' dominance, all because they held data security as sacrosanct. Their story wasn't just one of survival but of triumph over adversity, underscoring that adherence to best practices in data security is not just prudent—it's potentially transformative.

The journey doesn't end with selecting stellar software and establishing robust protocols. The digital landscape is perpetually shifting; what's secure today may be vulnerable tomorrow. Thus, **regular software updates and team education** on emerging threats become our navigational compasses in this journey. Reflect upon how even the most advanced fortifications can crumble without vigilant upkeep and learning. Our dedication to staying abreast of updates and educating our team is what keeps our defenses impregnable.

As we forge ahead in this digital era, let us take a moment to reflect on our role as custodians of financial data. The decisions we make today shape not just the immediate future but set the course for how securely we navigate the challenges ahead. By embodying these principles—selecting with care, practicing with diligence, and educating with fervor—we don't just protect data; we build legacies of trust and resilience.

Let this chapter serve as both a guidepost and an inspiration as you embark on securing your financial vault in the digital age. The path may be fraught with challenges, but armed with knowledge, vigilance, and an unwavering commitment to security and compliance, triumph is within reach. Here's to forging ahead with confidence, knowing that by prioritizing the safeguarding of our financial data, we pave the way for enduring success in this dynamic digital landscape.

Chapter 8: Cultivating Innovation: Fostering a Culture of Continuous Learning

In the early hours of a brisk spring morning, the city was just beginning to stir from its slumber. The gentle hum of awakening could be felt in the air, a subtle vibration that promised the start of something new. In a modest office building nestled among the giants of glass and steel, Julia sat in her corner cubicle, surrounded by ledgers and spreadsheets that seemed as ancient as the abacus.

She had always found solace in numbers; they were constant and true. But lately, each digit whispered of change, an insistent murmur that spoke of a future where adaptability would be currency. Julia's fingers paused over her keyboard, her gaze lost in the glow of dual monitors casting a pale light on stacks of financial reports.

The company had recently decided to implement new accounting software, an endeavor that promised efficiency but demanded new learning. Her colleagues' reactions ranged from cautious optimism to veiled anxiety—emotions she felt herself oscillating between. She remembered seminars attended and articles devoured on digital innovation's relentless march forward; now it was at her doorstep.

Her coffee grew cold beside her as she pondered how best to foster an environment where her team could thrive amidst these changes. The clack of keys from nearby cubicles punctuated her thoughts like distant thunder, reminding Julia that growth never came without its share of storms.

Lunchtime brought with it a bustle as coworkers gathered around tables with sandwiches and salads bought from street vendors below. Conversations ebbed and flowed around Julia like waves upon the shore, many touching upon the digital transformation their department was undergoing. She listened intently to their concerns and aspirations, weaving them into an invisible tapestry she hoped would soon envelop them all in confidence and competence.

As afternoon light waned into dusk, shadows stretched across Julia's desk while she crafted an email detailing upcoming training sessions designed not just to instruct but to inspire. She knew well enough that skill without will served little purpose; it was passion for progress that would ultimately drive their success.

With evening's approach and offices emptying around her, Julia stood by the window overlooking a city ablaze with lights—a testament to human ingenuity and ambition. Her reflection mingled with scenes from streets below where people continued their dance with daily life.

As she gathered her belongings to join them in their homeward drifts, Julia considered what tomorrow might bring—more uncertainty or perhaps clarity? Would they embrace this journey toward innovation together or would fear anchor them in place?

In this quiet moment before stepping out into the crisp night air, one question lingered: How does one kindle a flame within others so it becomes bright enough to illuminate even the darkest corners of doubt?

Embrace Change or Be Left Behind

In the swiftly evolving landscape of accounting, where digital innovations are not just advancements but necessities, fostering a culture of continuous learning is paramount. This transformative approach isn't merely about staying relevant; it's about leading the charge towards a future where your accounting department is not just a functional necessity but a hub of innovation and strategic insight. The digital shift in accounting demands more than just technical upgrades; it requires a mindset shift. **Understanding the importance of continuous learning** in adapting to these digital innovations is the first critical step.

To thrive in this digital era, accounting departments must move beyond traditional practices and embrace new technologies. This involves exploring methods to encourage technology adoption and skill development among staff. It's about creating an environment where growth, development, and innovation are not just encouraged but are integral to everyday practices. This doesn't happen overnight. It requires deliberate action, strategic planning, and most importantly, a commitment from every member of the team.

Creating such an environment starts with leadership. Leaders must lead by example, showing a willingness to learn and adapt. They should champion training programs, invest in new technologies, and foster an atmosphere where sharing best practices is the norm. This demonstrates to the team that growth is valued and that each member's development contributes significantly to the department's success.

But it's not just about adopting new technologies; it's about *embracing a mindset of curiosity*. Encouraging staff to ask questions, challenge processes, and seek better solutions cultivates an innovative spirit. This spirit can transform accounting practices from routine tasks to strategic activities that drive business forward.

Furthermore, learning how to create an environment that supports this culture is vital. It involves recognizing achievements, providing constructive feedback, and facilitating open communication. Each of these elements helps build a supportive community within the department where individuals feel valued and motivated to contribute their best work.

Real-world examples serve as powerful motivators. Sharing stories of how embracing new technologies or methodologies led to significant improvements or breakthroughs can inspire teams. These narratives underscore the tangible benefits of adopting a culture of continuous learning and innovation.

By fostering a culture that values growth and development, accounting departments can future-proof themselves against the rapid pace of digital change. It turns challenges into opportunities for improvement and innovation. As you navigate this journey, remember that every step taken towards cultivating this environment not only enhances your department's capabilities but also solidifies its role as a pivotal part of your organization's success story.

Embracing continuous learning is not just about keeping up; it's about setting the pace in a digital world where only those willing to adapt will thrive. Through strategic planning, investment in people and technology, and fostering an innovative culture, your accounting department can transform into a powerhouse of efficiency and strategic insight.

Continuous learning is not just a buzzword; it is a fundamental necessity in today's rapidly evolving digital landscape. The accounting profession, traditionally known for its stability and adherence to established practices, is now at a crossroads where embracing innovation is no longer optional but imperative for survival. Understanding the importance of continuous learning in adapting to digital innovations is crucial for accounting professionals looking to stay relevant and competitive in the industry. **By recognizing that learning is a lifelong journey rather than a destination, accounting professionals can equip themselves with the skills and knowledge needed to navigate the digital shift successfully.**

In the realm of accounting, technological advancements such as automation, artificial intelligence, and cloud computing are reshaping traditional processes and workflows. To thrive in this new environment, accountants must be willing to step out of their comfort zones and embrace new tools and methodologies. **Continuous learning enables accountants to stay ahead of the curve, anticipate industry trends, and proactively adapt to changing circumstances.** By fostering a culture of continuous learning within the accounting department, organizations can empower their staff to acquire new skills, experiment with emerging technologies, and explore innovative solutions to complex problems.

Embracing continuous learning also cultivates a growth mindset among accounting professionals. Instead of viewing challenges as insurmountable obstacles, individuals with a growth mindset see them as opportunities for learning and development. This shift in perspective fosters resilience, creativity, and adaptability—essential qualities for thriving in an ever-changing business landscape. **By encouraging staff to engage in ongoing training programs, attend industry conferences, and participate in knowledge-sharing initiatives, organizations can create a culture that values curiosity, experimentation, and continuous improvement.**

Moreover, continuous learning promotes collaboration and knowledge sharing within the accounting department. When team members are encouraged to exchange ideas, share best practices, and learn from each other's experiences, the collective intelligence of the group grows exponentially. **By leveraging the diverse skills and perspectives of team members**, organizations can foster innovation, drive efficiency gains, and achieve sustainable growth in an increasingly competitive market.

Embracing continuous learning is not just about acquiring new technical skills; it is about cultivating a mindset that values adaptability, creativity, and lifelong growth. By prioritizing continuous learning within the accounting department, organizations can future-proof their operations and position themselves as leaders in an era of digital transformation. Ready to explore methods to encourage technology adoption among your accounting staff? Let's delve into practical strategies for fostering innovation through skill development in the next section.

In today's fast-paced digital landscape, staying current with technological advancements is crucial for the success of any accounting department. Encouraging technology adoption and skill development among accounting staff is essential to ensure that the team remains competitive and efficient in their work. **By fostering a culture of continuous learning within the department, organizations can empower their employees to embrace new technologies and enhance their skill sets.**

One effective method to encourage technology adoption is through providing regular training sessions and workshops. These sessions can cover a range of topics, from basic software usage to advanced data analytics techniques. **By investing in the professional development of your staff, you not only increase their proficiency with new tools but also boost their confidence in using them.** Additionally, **creating a safe space for employees to ask questions and seek help when needed can alleviate any fears or uncertainties they may have about adopting new technologies.**

Another way to promote technology adoption is by leading by example. When management demonstrates a willingness to embrace new tools and processes, it sets a positive precedent for the rest of the team. By showcasing the benefits of these technologies firsthand, leaders can inspire their staff to follow suit. Moreover,

encouraging a collaborative environment where team members can share their experiences and best practices with different tools can foster a sense of camaraderie and mutual support.

Skill development among accounting staff goes hand in hand with technology adoption. Offering opportunities for employees to upskill or reskill not only benefits the individual but also strengthens the overall capabilities of the team. By identifying areas where additional training is needed and providing resources for further education, organizations can ensure that their staff are well-equipped to handle any challenges that arise.

Recognizing and rewarding employees who actively engage in technology adoption and skill development can also be a powerful motivator. By celebrating achievements and progress, organizations reinforce the importance of continuous learning and create a culture that values growth and improvement. This positive reinforcement encourages employees to continue expanding their knowledge and exploring new ways to enhance their performance.

In summary, **encouraging technology adoption and skill development among accounting staff is essential for maintaining a competitive edge in today's digital landscape. By investing in training programs, leading by example, fostering collaboration, offering opportunities for skill development, and recognizing employee efforts, organizations can create a culture that embraces innovation and continuous learning.**

In fostering a culture of continuous learning within the accounting department, creating an environment that supports growth, development, and innovation is paramount. **Encouraging staff to embrace new technologies and participate in training programs** is essential to staying ahead in the industry. By providing opportunities for skill development and knowledge enhancement, accounting professionals can adapt to digital innovations more effectively. **Supporting a culture of learning involves promoting collaboration** among team members, where sharing best practices and exchanging ideas become the norm.

To cultivate innovation in accounting practices, it's crucial to establish an environment that values curiosity and exploration. *Encouraging employees to ask questions, experiment with new tools, and seek out solutions* fosters a mindset of continuous improvement. By creating a space where **mistakes are viewed as learning opportunities**, rather than failures, individuals feel empowered to take risks and innovate.

Leaders within the accounting department play a significant role in shaping the culture of continuous learning. *By setting an example through their own commitment to growth and development*, managers can inspire their team members to do the same. **Providing resources and support for ongoing education** demonstrates a dedication to employee advancement and contributes to a culture that prioritizes learning.

In this environment of growth and innovation, **celebrating achievements and milestones** becomes essential. Recognizing individual efforts and team accomplishments reinforces the value of continuous learning within the organization. **By acknowledging progress**, both small and large, organizations can motivate their employees to continue striving for excellence in their work.

Building a supportive network within the accounting department further enhances the culture of continuous learning. *Encouraging mentorship relationships* allows for knowledge sharing between experienced professionals and newer team members. This collaboration not only fosters skill development but also strengthens bonds within the team, creating a sense of community centered around growth.

Ultimately, cultivating a culture that supports growth, development, and innovation in accounting practices requires a **commitment from both leadership and staff.** *By fostering an* *environment that values learning*, organizations can future-proof their accounting departments and ensure they remain adaptable in an ever-evolving digital landscape. Embracing change, encouraging experimentation, and celebrating progress are all key components of creating a culture that thrives on continuous improvement.

Embracing a culture of continuous learning within the accounting department is not just an option; it's a necessity in today's rapidly evolving digital landscape. Recognizing the importance of adapting to digital innovations ensures that your team remains at the forefront of the industry, equipped with the latest tools and methodologies to streamline operations and enhance efficiency.

Encouraging technology adoption and skill development among your accounting staff goes beyond traditional training programs. It involves creating a supportive environment where curiosity is celebrated, and learning is seen as a journey rather than a destination. By championing these values, you foster a team that's not only proficient in current technologies but also adaptable to future advancements.

Creating an environment that supports growth, development, and innovation is akin to planting a garden. Just as a garden requires nurturing, so does your team's ability to innovate and grow. This means providing them with the resources they need, offering opportunities for professional development, and encouraging the sharing of best practices. It's about creating a space where mistakes are viewed as learning opportunities, and success is celebrated collectively.

Embrace Challenges as Opportunities

Every challenge encountered along the way is an opportunity for growth. Personal anecdotes from industry leaders who have navigated digital shifts successfully underscore this point. They remind us that triumph over adversity is not just possible but probable with the right mindset and support system.

Remember, fostering a culture of continuous learning is not solely about adopting new technologies; it's about nurturing a mindset of perpetual growth and adaptation. This approach not only future-proofs your accounting department but also cultivates a team that's resilient, innovative, and ready to embrace whatever changes the future may bring.

Ask yourself, are you doing enough to encourage an atmosphere of continuous learning within your team? Reflect on this question, and consider how adopting even one or two strategies outlined in this chapter could significantly impact your team's dynamic and productivity.

In essence, cultivating innovation through continuous learning is more than a strategic advantage; it's a vital component of thriving in today's digital accounting landscape. By prioritizing learning and adaptability, you ensure your team is not just surviving but thriving amidst ongoing technological advancements. Let this be your call to action: foster an environment where continuous improvement is the norm, not the exception, thereby unlocking unparalleled efficiency and compliance in your accounting practices without breaking the bank.

Chapter 9: The Seamless Ledger: Revolutionizing Your Financial Data Management

In the heart of the city, where skyscrapers mingled with the heavens and the streets hummed a tune of perpetual motion, there sat an office. Within this temple to commerce, a man named Thomas wrestled with ledgers and figures that sprawled across his desk like a cityscape in their own right. The seamless ledger, an innovation as enigmatic as it was promising, lay at the forefront of his mind.

Thomas' hands danced across the keyboard with an urgency that betrayed his calm exterior. The air around him was thick with ambition and the faint buzz of fluorescent lights overhead. He recalled tales of financial management before digital solutions—tales of errors and erasers, late nights drowned in paper tides. The seamless ledger promised liberation from such ancient binds.

A breeze slipped through a barely-open window, carrying with it the scent of rain on concrete. It nudged at Thomas' consciousness, whispering temptations of fresh air and open spaces far removed from numerical confines. Yet he remained anchored to his chair by invisible chains forged from duty and necessity.

His colleagues spoke in hushed tones about innovation and efficiency as if they were holy grails to be pursued with devout fervor. Thomas too had dreams where numbers flowed like rivers without dams, where every transaction found its place with grace—a symphony orchestrated by unseen digital maestros.

The chatter around him faded as he delved deeper into thoughts about how to foster such a mindset within his team—a collective geared towards embracing change rather than shying away from its unfamiliar face. They stood on the brink of revolutionizing financial data management, but first they must step into the unknown.

As day yielded to dusk outside his windowpane, Thomas pondered whether their pursuit would lead them to tranquility or turmoil. Would they emerge as pioneers or simply dreamers chasing after wisps of cloud? What does it truly take for an organization to cross the threshold into a future where accounting systems are not just tools but allies?

Unlock the Future of Finance

In a world where digital transformation is no longer a choice but a necessity, the concept of the seamless ledger emerges as a beacon of innovation in financial data management. This transformative approach is not just about adopting new technologies; it's about revolutionizing how we think about and handle financial transactions and data. With the right mindset, tools, and strategies, organizations can achieve unparalleled efficiency, ensure compliance with ease, and secure peace of mind in their accounting practices. The journey towards a streamlined, future-ready accounting system is not only possible but imperative for enhanced financial management.

Grasping the Seamless Ledger

At its core, the seamless ledger represents a holistic shift in managing financial data—moving from fragmented and manual processes to a unified digital solution. The benefits are manifold: real-time access to financial data, reduced errors through automation, enhanced security features, and significant cost savings. But understanding these benefits is just the beginning. It's about seeing the seamless ledger not as an end goal but as an ongoing process of improvement and adaptation to changing financial landscapes.

Digital Solutions: Your Path to Streamlined Accounting

Adopting and integrating digital solutions into your accounting process may seem daunting at first glance. Yet, with a strategic approach, this transition can be smooth and highly rewarding. Start by evaluating your current processes: Where are the bottlenecks? What tasks are most time-consuming? From there, explore digital tools that address these specific issues. Remember, the goal is not to replace human insight but to enhance it with technology—freeing up valuable time for strategic thinking and decision-making.

Innovation: The Heartbeat of Efficiency

Fostering a mindset geared towards innovation and efficiency is crucial in managing financial transactions and data effectively. This doesn't mean chasing after every new trend or technology. Instead, it's about being open to new ideas, willing to experiment, and learning from both successes and failures. Real-world examples abound of companies that have transformed their accounting practices by embracing innovative solutions—whether it's leveraging cloud-based platforms for greater accessibility or utilizing AI for predictive analytics.

Embrace Change with Confidence

Change can be intimidating, especially when it involves complex systems like financial management. However, remember that every organization, regardless of size or industry, has the potential to revolutionize its accounting practices through the seamless ledger concept. It's not just about technology; it's about adopting a new perspective on what efficient financial management looks like in the digital age.

The Value of Strategic Thinking

Strategic thinking is indispensable when navigating the digital shift in accounting. It involves looking beyond immediate challenges to anticipate future opportunities and threats. By doing so, you can make informed decisions that align with your organization's long-term goals—ensuring that your move towards a seamless ledger is not just a temporary fix but a sustainable strategy for success.

In embracing the seamless ledger approach to financial data management, organizations unlock a world of possibilities—streamlined processes, enhanced accuracy, and strategic insights that were previously out of reach. The journey may require courage to venture into uncharted territory and resilience to overcome inevitable challenges along the way. Yet, with each step forward, you're not just transforming your accounting practices; you're paving the way for a more efficient, compliant, and future-ready business.

Reflect on Your Journey

As you contemplate integrating these principles into your own context, consider where you currently stand in your digital transformation journey. What steps can you take today towards a more seamless financial management system? How can fostering an innovative mindset help overcome barriers to change? Remember that every organization's path will be unique—but the destination remains the same: streamlined operations that propel your business forward in an ever-evolving digital landscape.

In the realm of financial management, the concept of the seamless ledger represents a significant shift in how organizations handle their data and transactions. The traditional methods of managing financial information can be cumbersome, time-consuming, and prone to errors. However, with the seamless ledger, a streamlined and efficient approach emerges, promising enhanced accuracy, compliance, and peace of mind in accounting practices.

The Benefits of Embracing the Seamless Ledger

Embracing the seamless ledger brings a multitude of benefits to the table. Imagine a world where your financial data is effortlessly integrated, updated in real-time, and easily accessible at your fingertips. No more sifting through piles of paperwork or navigating complex spreadsheets. *Efficiency* is at the core of this transformation – tasks that used to take hours can now be completed in minutes with the help of digital solutions.

Moreover, **compliance** becomes less of a burden when your financial data is meticulously organized and secure within a seamless ledger system. Say goodbye to the stress of audits or regulatory checks; with accurate and up-to-date information readily available, meeting compliance requirements becomes a breeze.

Another significant advantage lies in **strategic decision-making**. When your financial data is seamlessly managed and easily interpretable, you gain valuable insights into your organization's performance. This empowers you to make informed decisions promptly, driving growth and sustainability for your business.

Revolutionizing Financial Data Management: A Call to Action

As we delve deeper into the concept and benefits of the seamless ledger, it becomes evident that this transformative approach has the potential to revolutionize financial data management for organizations large and small. By embracing this shift towards efficiency, compliance, and strategic decision-making, businesses can unlock a world of possibilities in their accounting practices. Join us as we explore how to integrate digital solutions seamlessly into your financial processes for a streamlined and future-ready approach.

In the realm of financial management, the integration of digital solutions is not just a trend but a necessity for modern organizations striving for efficiency and accuracy. **Adopting digital tools** can significantly streamline accounting processes, reducing the likelihood of errors and saving valuable time. By embracing technology, businesses can transition from manual, error-prone methods to automated systems that enhance productivity and compliance.

Digital solutions offer a myriad of benefits, from real-time tracking of financial data to automated report generation. These tools can simplify complex tasks like reconciliation and data entry, allowing finance teams to focus on strategic decision-making rather than mundane administrative work. The seamless integration of digital software into existing accounting systems can revolutionize how financial data is managed, providing a more accurate and comprehensive overview of an organization's financial health.

When considering the adoption of digital solutions, it is essential for organizations to **assess their current processes** and identify areas where technology can bring about significant improvements. By conducting a thorough analysis of existing workflows and pain points, businesses can pinpoint where automation and digitization will have the most substantial impact. This targeted approach ensures that digital solutions are strategically implemented to address specific needs and challenges within the organization.

Moreover, **training and upskilling** employees in utilizing new digital tools are crucial for successful integration. Investing in training programs that familiarize staff with software functionalities can enhance efficiency and ensure a smooth transition to automated processes. By empowering employees with the necessary skills to leverage digital solutions effectively, organizations can maximize the benefits of technology adoption and drive continuous improvement in their financial data management practices.

In today's fast-paced business environment, **flexibility and scalability** are key considerations when selecting digital solutions for financial management. Organizations should opt for software that can adapt to evolving business needs and accommodate growth without requiring significant reconfiguration or replacement. Scalable digital tools enable businesses to future-proof their accounting processes, ensuring that they remain agile and competitive in a dynamic marketplace.

By embracing digital solutions in financial management, organizations pave the way for enhanced efficiency, accuracy, and compliance in their accounting practices. The seamless integration of technology into existing workflows not only streamlines processes but also empowers finance teams to make data-driven decisions with confidence. As businesses navigate the digital shift in accounting, the adoption of innovative tools becomes paramount in revolutionizing how financial data is managed for long-term success.

In the realm of financial data management, fostering a mindset geared towards innovation and efficiency is paramount to success. It's not merely about adopting new technologies but embracing a culture of continuous improvement and adaptation. **By cultivating an environment that encourages creativity and forward thinking,** organizations can stay ahead of the curve in managing financial transactions and data.

Innovation in financial management is not just about implementing the latest software or tools; it's about challenging traditional methods and seeking out better ways to achieve goals. By encouraging your team to think outside the box, you open up avenues for fresh ideas and solutions that can streamline processes and enhance accuracy. **Embracing innovation means being open to change, even if it means stepping out of your comfort zone.**

Efficiency goes hand in hand with innovation. **Streamlining processes, automating repetitive tasks, and optimizing workflows are all essential components of an efficient financial management system.** By eliminating manual entry errors and reducing time-consuming tasks, efficiency frees up resources that can be redirected towards more strategic initiatives.

To foster a mindset of innovation and efficiency, it's crucial to lead by example. Encourage your team to experiment with new ideas, reward creative problem-solving, and provide opportunities for professional development. **By creating a culture that values**

innovation and efficiency, you empower your team to take ownership of their work and strive for excellence in everything they do.

Continuous learning is also key to fostering a mindset of innovation and efficiency. Encourage your team to stay informed about industry trends, attend training sessions, and seek out opportunities for skill development. **By investing in your team's growth,** you not only equip them with the tools they need to succeed but also inspire them to push boundaries and explore new possibilities.

Remember, innovation is not a one-time event but an ongoing process. **Encourage regular brainstorming sessions, feedback loops, and collaborative problem-solving efforts** to keep the momentum going. **By fostering a culture of continuous improvement,** you ensure that your organization remains agile, adaptable, and ready to tackle any challenges that come its way.

In conclusion, embracing innovation and efficiency in managing financial transactions and data is not just about adopting new technology; it's about cultivating a mindset that values creativity, forward thinking, and continuous improvement. **By leading by example,** investing in your team's growth, and promoting a culture of innovation,** you set the stage for long-term success in financial data management.

Embracing the seamless ledger in financial data management is not just about keeping up with technology; it's about seizing the opportunity to revolutionize how we approach our accounting practices. The journey towards a streamlined accounting process, as we have explored, hinges on understanding the profound benefits of digital solutions, integrating these technologies effectively, and fostering a culture of innovation and efficiency.

The adoption of digital solutions offers more than just operational efficiency; it provides a pathway to compliance and peace of mind. Imagine being able to access accurate financial data at the click of a button, or better yet, having that information work for you in real-time to make informed business decisions. This isn't a distant reality but a tangible goal within reach for organizations willing to invest in the right technology.

Fostering a mindset geared towards innovation is equally crucial. Reflect on the stories shared, where individuals and companies triumphed over adversity by thinking differently about their financial management. These aren't mere anecdotes but testaments to what's possible when we embrace change and challenge the status quo. It's about seeing beyond the numbers and understanding the stories they tell us about our business operations and opportunities for growth.

As we move forward, let's ask ourselves: Are we merely keeping pace with technological advancements or are we leveraging these tools to truly transform our accounting practices? The shift towards a seamless ledger is not just a step but a leap into a future where financial management is no longer a chore but a strategic asset.

The essence of revolutionizing financial data management lies in recognizing that this transformation requires more than just adopting new software; it demands a holistic shift in how we perceive and engage with our financial systems. By embracing digital solutions, fostering an innovative mindset, and integrating these practices into our daily operations, we unlock unprecedented levels of efficiency and compliance.

Let this chapter serve as both inspiration and guidance for those ready to embark on this transformative journey. Remember, the path to revolutionizing your financial data management begins with a single step—a step towards embracing change, challenging conventional wisdom, and ultimately achieving a level of operational excellence that sets your organization apart.

Innovation, efficiency, compliance—these are not just buzzwords but the pillars upon which future-ready accounting systems are built. As you turn these pages and reflect on your own practices, consider how you can contribute to shaping an environment where seamless ledgers are not just envisioned but realized with confidence and expertise.

Chapter 10: Embracing Change: The Roadmap to Digital Transformation in Accounting

The morning sun filtered through the blinds, casting a lattice of light and shadow across the mahogany desk where Michael sat, surrounded by ledgers and financial reports. His office bore the scent of aged paper and faint traces of coffee from the mug that sat beside him, steam rising in a slow dance. The digital clock on his wall ticked in steady rhythm, a counterpoint to the tap-tap-tap of fingers on a keyboard.

Michael's mind was awash with thoughts of transformation. The accounting firm he had built from scratch was at a crossroads, and he knew it was time to shed the skin of old methods. He recalled conversations with peers who had navigated similar paths, their words echoing promises of streamlined operations and improved efficiency through digitalization.

His gaze drifted to the window where the city below bustled with life; people were small dots from this height but each carried their own stories, their own resistance to change or embrace of it. He understood them. Change was daunting - an unknown expanse stretching beyond the horizon of his comfort zone.

In his chest, a thrumming heart battled between excitement for what could be and fear of missteps. The steps for initiating digital transformation seemed clear: assess current processes, identify technologies that could automate manual tasks, strategically plan for integration, ensure organizational readiness. Yet within each step lay challenges as intricate as the patterns sunlight made upon his desk.

He rose from his chair and walked to the window, pressing a hand against the cool glass as if to connect with the world outside. There were employees out there who relied on him; clients who trusted him with their financial wellbeing. His decision would ripple through lives like waves upon water.

A knock at his door pulled him back into reality. It was Lisa, one of his most adept accountants. "We're ready for your final review on the Thompson account," she said with an eager smile that belied her own trepidation about what digital transformation might mean for her role.

"Thank you, Lisa," Michael replied, offering a nod that masked his internal deliberations. "I'll be there shortly."

As he followed her out into the hall lined with doors behind which numbers were crunched and reports generated by human hands—for now—he pondered whether they all felt it too: this blend of anticipation and anxiety at standing on the precipice of change.

Would they grasp this opportunity firmly or let it slip like sand through fingers? Would they become architects of their future or relics in an ever-evolving landscape? And what unforeseen challenges lay in wait along this path they were about to tread?

Michael paused outside Lisa's office door; inside awaited figures that told stories not just of profits and losses but also hinted at futures yet unwritten. In those numbers lay both promise and warning—a map to guide them if only they dared follow it.

What would be discovered when tradition gave way to innovation?

The Future is Now: Navigating Your Path Through Digital Transformation

As we stand at the cusp of a new era in accounting, the move from traditional, manual processes to automated, digital systems is not just an option; it's an imperative. The journey towards digital transformation in accounting represents a monumental shift, introducing efficiencies and accuracies previously unattainable. This chapter serves as your compass, guiding you through the essential steps to initiate this transformation, plan strategically for technology integration, and foster organizational readiness for continuous improvement.

The first step in this transformative journey is to **recognize the essential steps for initiating digital transformation** in your accounting processes. It begins with a comprehensive assessment of your current practices to pinpoint areas ripe for improvement through digital intervention. Setting clear objectives for what you aim to achieve—be it enhanced efficiency, accuracy, or compliance—is crucial. These goals lay the groundwork for a timeline segmented into manageable phases, complemented by Key Performance Indicators (KPIs) that track progress and measure success.

Moving forward requires strategic planning for **the integration of modern accounting technologies**. This involves researching and selecting digital solutions that align with your objectives. Crafting a detailed implementation plan is next, detailing steps, resources, timelines, and preparing for potential challenges. Allocating both financial and human resources underscores the commitment to not just adopt new technologies but to integrate them seamlessly into existing systems.

Understanding **the critical importance of organizational readiness** cannot be overstated. It's about bringing everyone on board—communicating the vision and objectives across all levels of the organization to ensure alignment and support. Cultivating a culture that prizes continuous improvement is essential; it turns feedback into actionable insights for optimization. Providing training ensures employees can leverage new technologies effectively, while regular reviews assess impacts and refine strategies.

The Roadmap Unveiled: Your Blueprint for Success

Step 1: Launching Your Digital Voyage

- Begin with a thorough review of existing processes to identify digital enhancement opportunities.

- Clearly define your transformation goals and segment your timeline into feasible phases.

- Establish KPIs to monitor progress and success.

Estimated Timeframe: 1-2 Months

Step 2: Strategic Planning & Technology Integration

- Select digital tools that meet your outlined goals.
- Develop an exhaustive plan detailing implementation steps.
- Allocate necessary resources and prepare for potential hurdles.

Estimated Timeframe: 2-3 Months

Step 3: Building Organizational Fortitude

- Communicate the transformation vision clearly across all stakeholders.
- Foster an environment conducive to continuous learning and improvement.
- Invest in training and regularly review transformation impacts.

Estimated Timeframe: 1 Month (Ongoing)

Success in this journey doesn't merely lie in reaching the destination but in navigating the pathway with agility and foresight. By embracing these steps, organizations can unlock unparalleled efficiency and compliance in their accounting practices without being bogged down by complexity or cost.

Throughout "The Seamless Ledger," we've explored how daunting manual accounting processes can lead to errors and inefficiencies. This chapter ties together themes of automation, cloud computing, data analysis, regulatory compliance, fraud prevention, training, and outsourcing as integral components of streamlining accounting processes. By embarking on this roadmap to digital transformation, organizations are equipped not just for a transition but for a profound evolution towards more efficient, accurate, and compliant financial management.

Remember, embracing change is not just about adopting new technologies; it's about fostering a mindset that welcomes innovation as a constant companion on the road to progress. As you embark on this journey of digital transformation in accounting, let strategic planning be your map and organizational readiness your vehicle towards achieving seamless financial operations that stand resilient in the face of tomorrow's challenges.

Digital transformation in accounting is not just a buzzword; it's a crucial shift towards efficiency, accuracy, and compliance in financial processes. To initiate this transformation successfully, there are essential steps that organizations must recognize and implement. **First and foremost**, acknowledging the need for change is vital. Understanding that manual processes are time-consuming, error-prone, and inefficient is the initial step towards embracing digital transformation. It's about realizing that there is a better way to handle accounting tasks, one that can streamline operations and enhance overall performance.

Once the recognition phase is complete, the next step involves assessing the current state of affairs within the organization. Conducting a thorough audit of existing processes, identifying pain points, and pinpointing areas where automation can make a significant impact is crucial. This assessment sets the foundation for developing a strategic plan for digital transformation. **By understanding where**

improvements are needed, organizations can tailor their approach to match their unique requirements and goals.

Following the assessment, it's essential to define clear objectives for the digital transformation journey. Establishing measurable goals allows organizations to track progress effectively and stay focused on achieving tangible outcomes. Whether the aim is to reduce processing time, minimize errors, or enhance data analysis capabilities, having clear objectives provides a roadmap for success. **Setting achievable milestones** along the way can help maintain momentum and ensure continuous progress towards the desired transformation.

One of the key elements in initiating digital transformation in accounting is securing buy-in from stakeholders across the organization. Change management plays a significant role in ensuring successful implementation of new technologies and processes. **By involving key stakeholders early on**, addressing concerns, and communicating the benefits of digital transformation, organizations can create a supportive environment for change. Engaging employees at all levels fosters a sense of ownership and commitment to the transformation process.

Embracing Change: The Catalyst for Progress

In embracing change lies the catalyst for progress. It's not just about adopting new technologies but also about fostering a culture that values innovation, efficiency, and continuous improvement. By recognizing the essential steps for initiating digital transformation in accounting processes, organizations pave the way for a more streamlined, agile approach to financial management. The journey towards digital transformation begins with awareness, assessment, goal-setting, and stakeholder engagement—a roadmap that leads towards enhanced efficiency, accuracy, and compliance in accounting practices.

In the pursuit of digital transformation in accounting, strategic planning for the integration of modern technologies is paramount. **Successful implementation requires a clear roadmap,** outlining the steps needed to transition from traditional methods to efficient, automated processes. Begin by assessing your current accounting practices and identifying areas that would benefit most from technological upgrades. Consider the pain points in your workflow, such as manual data entry or lack of real-time insights, and prioritize solutions that address these challenges.

Research and select appropriate accounting software that aligns with your business needs and goals. Look for platforms that offer automation features, cloud-based accessibility, and robust security measures. Engage with vendors to understand the capabilities of the software and how it can streamline your financial operations. Remember, investing in technology is an investment in the future efficiency of your accounting processes.

Develop a detailed implementation plan that outlines timelines, responsibilities, and milestones for each phase of the digital transformation journey. Collaborate with key stakeholders within your organization to ensure alignment and commitment to the transition. Communication is key during this phase; keep all team members informed about the changes ahead, addressing any concerns or resistance proactively.

As you progress towards integrating modern accounting technologies, **prioritize training and upskilling** for your team members. Equip them with the knowledge and skills needed to leverage new tools effectively. Offer hands-on workshops, online tutorials, or external training resources to support their learning journey. A well-trained team is essential for maximizing the benefits of digital transformation and ensuring a smooth transition.

Monitor progress regularly, reviewing key performance indicators (KPIs) to track the impact of technology integration on your accounting processes. Identify areas of improvement and adjust your strategies accordingly. Embrace a culture of continuous learning and adaptation within your organization, fostering innovation and agility in response to changing business landscapes.

As you navigate the roadmap towards digital transformation in accounting, **embrace flexibility** in your approach. Technology evolves rapidly, and new solutions may emerge that could enhance your financial processes further. Stay informed about industry trends and emerging technologies, remaining open to exploring new possibilities for optimizing your accounting practices.

In summary, strategic planning for integrating modern accounting technologies is a crucial step towards achieving digital transformation in accounting. By assessing your needs, selecting suitable software, developing a detailed implementation plan, prioritizing training for your team, monitoring progress, and embracing flexibility, you can pave the way for a more efficient and streamlined financial operation in the digital era.

Conceptual Model in Systems Theory

To successfully navigate the digital transformation journey in accounting, it is crucial to adopt a Conceptual Model in Systems Theory that focuses on the organization as a dynamic system undergoing change. This model encompasses various components that work together to drive the transformation process forward, ensuring efficiency, compliance, and scalability.

Inputs:

The inputs of the model include the organization's **current state**, **available resources**, and **readiness for digital transformation**. Understanding where the organization stands in terms of its technological capabilities, human resources, and willingness to embrace change is essential for laying the groundwork for successful transformation.

System Processes:

The system processes within the model encompass **strategic planning**, **stakeholder engagement**, **technology selection**, and **implementation**. Strategic planning involves setting clear objectives and outlining a roadmap for implementation. Stakeholder engagement ensures buy-in from all involved parties, fostering a collaborative approach to change. Technology selection involves identifying and implementing the right tools to support digital transformation, while implementation focuses on executing the planned changes effectively.

Outputs:

The desired outputs of the model include increased **efficiency**, **compliance**, **scalability**, and improved **financial decision-making capabilities**. These outcomes signify the successful integration of digital technologies into the accounting processes, leading to enhanced performance and better decision-making abilities.

Feedback Loops:

Feedback loops play a critical role in the model by enabling continuous refinement and adaptation of the transformation process. By gathering feedback on outcomes and adjusting strategies based on evolving organizational needs or goals, the model ensures that digital transformation remains aligned with the organization's objectives.

By aligning organizational change with systems thinking, this Conceptual Model in Systems Theory provides a comprehensive view of the variables, processes, and feedback mechanisms that influence successful digital transformation in accounting. It emphasizes a holistic approach to change management, highlighting the interconnectedness of different components within an organization undergoing transformation.

Embracing the digital transformation in accounting is not just about adopting new technologies; it's about reshaping the very foundation of how financial operations are conducted. The journey, as outlined, demands a strategic approach, a willingness to invest in cutting-edge solutions, and an unwavering commitment to continuous improvement. This transition from manual to automated processes represents a significant shift that requires both organizational readiness and a mindset geared towards embracing change.

Recognizing the essential steps for initiating digital transformation is crucial. It sets the stage for a successful transition by ensuring that every action taken is aligned with the broader objectives of efficiency, accuracy, and compliance. It's about making informed decisions that propel your organization forward in the digital landscape.

Strategic planning for the integration of modern accounting technologies cannot be overstated. It serves as your roadmap, guiding each step of your journey towards digitalization. This planning involves not only identifying which technologies will bring about the most significant benefits but also understanding how they will fit into your existing processes and what adjustments will need to be made.

The **importance of organizational readiness and commitment to continuous improvement** in this digital era is fundamental. Change is constant, and the ability to adapt quickly and efficiently sets apart successful organizations from the rest. This readiness involves fostering a culture that values innovation, encourages experimentation, and learns from setbacks.

The narrative of our book underscores a profound truth: in the face of overwhelming complexity and the daunting task of manual accounting management, there lies a path to simplicity, efficiency, and compliance. Through practical tools and comprehensive knowledge provided herein, you are now equipped to streamline your accounting processes within a realistic timeframe—without being overwhelmed by complexity or cost.

Remember, every anecdote shared and every piece of advice given has been aimed at inspiring you to take bold steps towards transforming your accounting practices. You're not alone on this journey; many have navigated this path before you, turning challenges into triumphs through perseverance, strategic thinking, and an entrepreneurial spirit.

As we draw this discussion to a close, reflect on how far you've come and how much closer you are to achieving a seamless ledger. The integration of technology within your accounting practices isn't just a goal; it's a continuous journey towards excellence. Your commitment to embracing change, learning from every step, and striving for improvement will ensure that you not only navigate the digital shift in accounting with ease but also thrive in it.

Embrace this journey with an open mind and heart. Let innovation be your guide as you unlock new possibilities for efficiency and compliance in your accounting practices. Here's to navigating the digital shift with confidence and emerging stronger on the other side.

Epilogue

Embracing the Future: The Seamless Transition to Digital Accounting

As we draw the curtain on this transformative journey, it's essential to reflect on the profound changes that digital technologies bring to the accounting profession. The world of numbers, once confined within the walls of ledgers and files, now stretches infinitely within the digital realm. This book has navigated you through the labyrinth of digital accounting, demystifying complex concepts and presenting practical solutions to age-old problems. Together, we've explored how embracing technology not only enhances efficiency and compliance but also opens up a world of opportunities for those willing to take the leap.

The real-world applications of digital accounting are boundless, from small businesses seeking growth to multinational corporations aiming for global dominance. The strategies and tools discussed here are not mere theories but are battle-tested methods designed to bring about tangible improvements in your accounting practices. By adopting these innovations, you're not just keeping up with the times; you're setting a new standard for excellence in your field.

Remember, at its core, this transition is about **simplifying processes**, enhancing **accuracy**, and ensuring **compliance**—all while keeping costs in check. Whether it's through automation, cloud computing, or data analytics, the goal remains the same: to make your life easier and your business more profitable.

To truly benefit from this digital shift, I encourage you to start small. Identify one or two areas within your accounting practices that could use improvement and explore digital solutions that address those needs. It's about taking that first step with confidence and curiosity, knowing that each small victory brings you closer to a future where financial management is not just a necessity but a strategic advantage.

It's important to acknowledge that no journey is without its challenges. As much as we've covered in these pages, there's always more to learn, more to explore. The landscape of digital accounting is ever-evolving, with new technologies emerging and regulations changing. Staying informed and adaptable is key to navigating this dynamic environment successfully.

So, as you close this book and look towards implementing these insights into your work or business, remember that change is a process, not an event. It requires patience, perseverance, and a willingness to learn from both successes and setbacks. But most importantly, it requires you—a visionary willing to chart a new course for financial excellence.

In closing, I leave you with an empowering thought from Nelson Mandela: "It always seems impossible until it's done." Let this be a reminder that no goal is too lofty if approached with determination and guided by knowledge. Your journey toward seamless digital accounting may seem daunting now, but armed with the insights from this book and a steadfast resolve, there's no limit to what you can achieve.

"It always seems impossible until it's done." - Nelson Mandela

Did you love *The Seamless Ledger: Navigating the Digital Shift in Accounting*? Then you should read *Compass for the Soul: Navigating Life's Journey with Lessons from Jesus*[1] by Tommy George!

[2]

Imagine finding yourself at a crossroads in life, where the path ahead feels uncertain, and the road behind seems faded with the footprints of conformity. If you resonate with this sense of seeking clarity amidst the chaos of modern society, then you are the ideal reader for "Compass for the Soul: Navigating Life's Journey with Lessons from Jesus." You may be a young adult grappling with the turmoil of transitioning into adulthood, fervently upholding your values amidst societal pressures. Perhaps you are facing personal adversities, yearning for meaningful relationships, and thirsting for spiritual fulfillment. Your heart beats with a deep longing for growth, resilience, and an unwavering desire

1. https://books2read.com/u/bQGKED
2. https://books2read.com/u/bQGKED

to discover a purpose that aligns with your core being. As you read through the pages of this book, you will find solace and guidance in the stories of Jesus, drawing parallels to your own journey of personal development. The ancient wisdom shared within these pages will illuminate a path towards overcoming adversity, fostering resilience, and igniting faith in the face of your struggles. Through introspection and reflection, you will embark on a transformative voyage of self-discovery, uncovering your unique mission in the tapestry of existence. As you delve deeper into the teachings inspired by Jesus, you will cultivate meaningful relationships, kindle the flames of compassion, and forge a stronger spiritual connection, ultimately finding your place and purpose in this chaotic yet beautiful world. Let this book be your beacon of light in the darkness, your compass guiding you through the stormy seas of uncertainty. Embrace the wisdom of the ages intertwined with the struggles of today, and watch as you unravel the layers of doubt and confusion to reveal the gem of your true essence. With each turn of the page, may you inch closer to a more profound understanding of yourself, your purpose, and your role in this grand tapestry of life. So, dear reader, take this journey with an open heart, a curious mind, and a yearning spirit, for within these words lies the key to unlocking the treasure trove of your soul's purpose

Also by Tommy W. George

Soul-Tech: Exploring the Intersection of Technology and Spirituality
The Art Of Radical Thanksgiving
Compass for the Soul: Navigating Life's Journey with Lessons from Jesus
The Seamless Ledger: Navigating the Digital Shift in Accounting
Digital Shepherd: Leading with Heart and Pixels in a Connected Congregation

About the Author

Tommy W. George is the founder and Pastor of Praise Chapel International, Virginia, USA He is a successful entrepreneur, having established and owned two business. He is also an accountant. He was born in Liberia, the western part of Africa, before he finally move to the United Sates due to the Liberian civil unrest. He is married to Martine A. George, with four kids.

www.ingramcontent.com/pod-product-compliance
Lightning Source LLC
LaVergne TN
LVHW090418210926
848480LV00002B/612